D1488264

STRATEGIC ALTERNATIVES

STRATEGIC ALTERNATIVES

Selection, Development, and Implementation

William E. Rothschild

amacom

A Division of American Management Associations

Library of Congress Cataloging in Publication Data

Rothschild, William E
  Strategic alternatives.

  Includes index.
    1. Corporate planning.   2. Management.   1. Title.
  HD30.28.R67   658.4'01   79-11194
  ISBN 0-8144-5514-X

© 1979 AMACOM
A division of American Management Associations, New
York. All rights reserved. Printed in the United States of
America.

First Printing

To Alma, my loving wife,
without whom this book would
never have been written

PREFACE

FOR the past seven years, I have spent hundreds of hours consulting with general managers, strategic planners, and even chief executive officers of small, medium, and large corporations. This effort was aimed at helping them develop strategic plans and apply the principles of strategic thinking. As a result of these personal experiences, and on the basis of discussing these topics with other practitioners, I have become concerned about the lack of creativity and of true strategic alternatives in management. Managements have been willing to analyze their environments, competition, and resources, and have committed considerable organizational time, money, and personnel only to come up with the same old answers or with slight modifications of their existing strategy.

"Why?" I've asked. Why won't managements finish the job and demand more of themselves and of their subordinates? The answer is complex. First of all, generating alternatives is complicated, difficult, and even a bit frightening— complicated because it takes considerable time and effort to develop options; difficult because it requires new insights and a willingness to look at the problem from a variety of angles instead of from the same perspective; and frightening because it may require admitting that your past and current strategy won't work in the future and because it may require a personal change, more risk, or even a recognition that a new management is necessary.

These are difficult problems to resolve, and I won't pretend that this book addresses these areas. However, there is a less complicated but more pervasive reason that alternatives are not generated, and I *will* discuss this—namely, management may not even recognize that options exist which can fit their business situation. Furthermore, even if management does recognize that options exist, it may not understand what it will take to successfully implement the alternatives.

This book is designed to enable you, the reader, to recognize the large number of strategic alternatives that have been successfully used, and to increase your insight into these options, when they will and will not work, and what they will require to succeed. Since I believe that examples and illustrations clarify concepts and increase understanding, I have tried to provide true-to-life examples taken from recent public documents.

I have also provided a means of translating investment and management strategies into functional strategies, so that each functional executive can understand that it is a critical part of making strategic plans viable. This is called implementation strategy. Another failing that I have observed in the past: quite often, creative alternatives have been developed and documented but were only partially implemented, because functional managers never felt committed to their implementation or, if they were committed, they didn't know how to convert these strategic alternatives into action programs.

This book is aimed at stimulating your creativity, helping you select the most appropriate alternative, and then showing you how to convert it into implementation strategies and programs. If properly used, this book will help you develop additional alternatives. This is what the book *is*—an aid and stimulus. But let me also emphasize what the book *is not:* It is not a cookbook or a menu of strategies that can be picked out and implemented indiscriminately or without a thorough analysis of your environment, competition, and resources. It will only be an effective and valuable aid if *you* do the total thinking and planning job. For this reason, I have provided a review of the critical steps required to develop a strategy. This can help make the difference between successful strategic planning and planning that is less successful and that even wastes valuable managerial time and effort.

To say that the world is changing would be an understatement. The key is to recognize that you can't rest on your past accomplishments; you *must* be responsive and consider other ways to operate your business in the future. Those other ways are the essence of strategic alternatives.

William E. Rothschild

CONTENTS

1 Strategy: An Overview   1

Part I   Strategic Thinking and Decisions

2 Highlights of Strategic Thinking   17
3 Making Decisions and Setting Priorities   44

Part II   Successful Management Strategies

4 Marketing-Based Strategies   75
5 Production-Based Strategies   104
6 Innovation: The Glamour Strategy   123
7 Using Financing and Executive Talents   146

Part III   Functional Decisions and Total Strategy Integration

8 Implementation Strategies   167
9 The Final Steps   200
10 Conclusions and Directions for Use   224

Index   227

1

Strategy:
An Overview

"I plan to aggressively pursue this new market by innovation, which will enable me to use my current distribution and strong cash position." This is a simple strategic statement that highlights the investment, management, and implementation strategy decisions that must be made. It gives direction to the business team and implies certain market and financial results. In this chapter, I would like to outline the various strategic alternatives that could be followed. In later chapters, I shall elaborate on the nature of these alternatives and when they should be considered, and give examples of those companies in which they have been used.

Three key decisions underlie the operation of every successful enterprise:

—Where, how much, and why to invest? This is called an *investment* level of strategy and requires the chief executive officer to decide which business or segment of a business

Figure 1-1. The three key strategies.

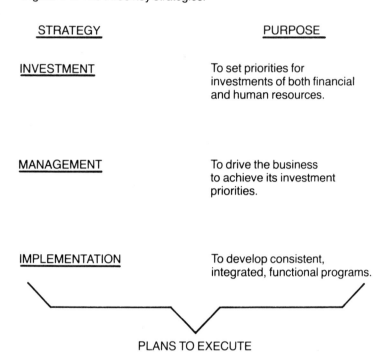

should be given the biggest portion of capital, cash, and managerial commitment.

—What will be the leading *thrust* or *driver* of this investment strategy? This may be product-innovative, marketing-, manufacturing-, finance-, or executive-based. I call this strategic decision a *management* strategy.

—What is expected of each functional area of the business? What are the crucial programs, and will they require a company to take a totally new approach or to obtain skills and resources that are not presently available? This I call *implementation* strategy.

Figure 1–1 illustrates these three fundamental levels of decision-making. Throughout this book, these options will be discussed and related to the other strategic decisions that need to be made in order to formulate a viable and comprehensive strategy.

Investment Strategy

There are five fundamental investment strategies available to businesses today. Investments can be made for the purpose of *growth* or to *penetrate* a market; to *hold* or *defend* one's position; to *rebuild;* to *harvest* the rewards of past investments; or to *exit* from a market (*divestment*). *Penetration* and *growth* are the objectives of many entrepreneurs. They are the kinds of strategies that are written about and lauded, especially when they are successful. Their aim is to increase volume and sales dollars either by improving market share or by adding to the sales base of other markets, market segments, or even of new industries. At times management even creates new markets or develops demand that substitutes for another market. At other times, this growth is merely achieved by serving markets that were previously considered outside the company's scope. For instance, an exclusively American company moves into Europe, or Mexico, or even the Far East. This action normally requires investment beyond immediate rewards. Sales grow, but income will normally lag, and cash will be required from other sources. If we were mathematicians we would say that Sales Growth is greater than Income and Cash Growth, or Sales Δ > Income Δ. Thus investment strategies aimed at growth require long-term commitment and a willingness to assume risks and wait for the payoff.

Holding and *defending* are normally the choice of the current leader, the company that already has the largest market share. Sales may grow, but that is usually because the market is growing, not because the company is aggressive. However, there are times when a follower may also choose this option—primarily when he is content with his current position, when he is making satisfactory profits, or when he realizes that the cost of gaining share or moving into strange markets is higher than he wishes to pay. This doesn't mean that defending is always easy or inexpensive. There are times when costs are high because a new company is entering the market or because an existing company has decided to become more aggressive. For example, traditional watch manufacturers had to invest in new technologies or reduce the prices of their products to ward off the invasion of their market by integrated circuit and liquid crystal technology. Normally, holding and defense strategies are aimed at increasing profits, and in this case profit growth usually exceeds sales growth. As a market matures, this is the most desirable position for a company.

Rebuilding is the option of the onetime leader who has given up position—or, as we say, "sold share"—either because of complacency or because of the desire for short-term profits. A turnaround or rebuilding strategy can be expensive and difficult, even impossible. It may be more costly than growth, and it should only be followed if the business or segment is important for other reasons. For instance, a particular segment may be needed for the company to be considered a "full-line producer," or because the customer requires participation and a weak position isn't economical. I would normally recommend divestment and focusing on new businesses or segments. The financial and market characteristics of rebuilding are similar to those of penetration or growth strategies.

Harvesting can be highly desirable as well as very rewarding, and it is as inevitable as old age. Most managements *falsely* equate harvesting with surrender. Harvesting often contributes cash and profits that can be invested elsewhere. In this situation, a company invests less money than it receives and is in a positive cash position. Harvesting is typical of leaders in maturing and declining markets, where the rewards of past investment are now being reaped. Every company should have part of its business portfolio in this category, and should work hard to reap the benefits gradually.

Exit/divestment strategies should be rare, but they should not be disregarded. Here, management recognizes the inevitable and decides to get out quickly and channel its efforts and resources elsewhere. If properly executed, exit strategies can be used to pay for growth or for a holding strategy in another division of the company. Timing is the key to this option: If you pull out too soon, you may not get rewards; if you leave too late, you may wind up with excessive losses. In an exit strategy, obviously sales are hurt, but cash flows can be attractive, and positive income may be realized. Although I most often equate this option with *no* investment, it may not be so. At times a planned exit may require some investment to obtain top dollar. For example, a homeowner wishing to sell his home may invest in paint and some gardening to make his property more attractive and thus get a better price. So, too, a businessman may invest in gaining some new market share or in improving his plant to make the buyer eager to purchase.

A key point to remember is that are many investment options and that every businessman should evaluate *each* segment or line, to determine which investment strategy is most appropriate for that particular segment. Thus, a total business investment strategy may be directed toward growth, holding, or harvesting, but will have some segments oriented toward one mode and others toward other modes.

Management Strategy—the Thrust or Driver

But strategy doesn't stop with a decision "to invest or not to invest"; it requires a decision as to how. Will growth be achieved by innovation, marketing, manufacturing, finance, or executive actions? Will it be based on self-development, acquisition, or joint venture? This decision leads to the selection of a *management strategy*. Have you ever noticed that the companies that really make it are noted for some major thrust? For instance, Procter and Gamble is considered a "marketing/product-planning" company, and when it elects to grow or defend its position, it does so by developing a differentiated product and promoting it extensively. Du Pont is usually innovative, starting with a unique product or process or developing a new substitute material, and then moving aggressively into the market. Other companies are noted for cost efficiency, and still others add capacity to penetrate even before they are certain that the market will grow.

At this point it should be emphasized once again that segments will vary and that a management strategy selected for one may be inappropriate for another. So, even though Du Pont is considered innovative, that doesn't mean that it exercises this thrust in every segment. Companies often have a portfolio of management as well as of investment strategies.

Marketing-driven strategies are often equated with the packaged goods industry (soap, detergents, cereal, canned foods), where short-term opportunities are created and capitalized upon quickly, usually through extensive advertising and promotion. This is often referred to as a "pull" strategy, since it *pulls* the consumer into the store to buy the product.

But marketing strategies are more than just promotional. I have seen situations in which the key problem was to get the customer to be able to *use* the product. For example, if a customer rents one of your computers and pays only for the time he uses it, then you would want to increase his usage. This may require "application" development and demonstration. This approach proved highly successful for IBM, which provided "application" salesmen to show how the computer could be used for technological problems, for accounting, scheduling, controlling inventory, and so on.

Other marketing strategies are aimed not at promotion or application, but at making the product readily available. Consumers or industrial companies have no difficulty obtaining the product or knowing where the product can be acquired. This is called a distribution/deployment/readiness-to-serve strategy. It may involve unique stocking plans, and extensive distributor or dealer networks.

Service can also be a major driver before, during, or after sales service. For instance, a customer group may require assurance that repairs will be made readily, economically, and effectively (e.g., utilities demand for power generation repair). Here the driving force is the customer's confidence that you can fix the equipment to minimize down time. This strategy is particularly important in highly capital-intensive industries where utilization is critical to the customer's success.

Finally, marketing-driven strategies may be determined purely by price. Setting the lowest price—or, in some cases, the highest price—has proved to be the secret to many companies' success. In my discussion of this strategy I shall elaborate on the different versions of pricing strategies that are available regardless of whether the desire is to grow, hold, harvest, or exit.

Innovation-based strategies, those based on product or technology innovation, also offer a variety of choices. A company may decide to become the leader and displace the competitors by devising an entirely new concept or approach—for instance, using solar-driven generators in place of those powered by gas or oil. This approach is costly and highly risky, but if it works, the rewards can be extensive and can even continue over long periods of time; witness the success of Xerox and Polaroid. Normally the lead provides patent protection, and this can be enough to provide a "leg up" for 17 years.

Another innovation-based strategy focuses on product or service differentiation. In this case, the company attempts to create a *real* difference in the product which enables it to develop a customer preference. This difference may be found in either the quality or reliability of the product, or can be obtained merely by adding style or special features. This is commonly done in the automobile industry. High-priced cars try to project the image of high quality and reliability; others merely appear to be different, because they have a unique grill, window shape, or fender design. Product differentiation based on appearance is difficult to sustain and protect, whereas differentiation based on *real* performance, reliability, or quality tends to have a more lasting value.

Product-innovation strategies can also be based on making the company's product or approach the industry standard. Standardization permits a firm to reap the value of quantity runs and mass production techniques and often provides ad-

ditional licensing income. At times this approach can give a
company the opportunity to sell accessories, components, and
replacement parts. Another, more marketing-oriented form
of standardization may try to make stereo available to the
average consumer rather than to the audiophile, or attempt
to develop a sports car for the mass market.
Many companies have used their manufacturing and processing know-how to grow, hold, protect, or even decrease
their position. This is known as a *production-based* or
manufacturing-based strategy. Capacity utilization and addition
strategies are very popular in capital-intensive industries in
which utilization rates are critical. For instance, in the paper
industry, 85–90% utilization is critical to profitability. In some
complex and long–lead-time industries, capacity addition
prior to and in anticipation of demand has proved successful,
though risky. If the demand forecasts are accurate and the
demand materializes on schedule, then the company with the
on-line ability to serve the market can reap handsome rewards.

Process or procedure improvements aimed at efficiency
and productivity are also common. They may take the form
of increased automation to permit long, less costly runs; or
they may be aimed at developing special equipment that can
consistently meet tight tolerances; or they may take the form
of increasing flexibility which, in turn, will permit short runs
and special designs. Each of these options can be effective in
helping a company gain share or improve its earnings.

A third form of production-based strategy emphasizes the
supply side of the production cycle. In this case the strategy
may be aimed at assuring supply or reducing costs. In other
cases the company may try to reduce capital needs or increase
flexibility by buying components or even complete products
rather than by manufacturing them itself. I have known companies that have competed successfully for years without ever
making a single product. This kind of strategy is commonly
referred to as a "sourcing" strategy, since the product is
sourced from a manufacturer but sold under the buyer's
brand.

Making, marketing, and innovating a product aren't the

only strategic choices; there are other finance-based strategies. For instance, you can create a barrier against competition by establishing a "leasing versus acquisition" approach, wherein you create a barrier by requiring extensive cash to participate in the market. This, in turn, can force out those who can provide the required cash. Special terms and conditions can serve the same purpose—for example, providing long-term, low-interest loans. This has been very effective in international sales. In recent years, franchising with equity ownership has also been a successful means of creating new markets or of assuring consistency and quality. Another effective approach is consignment selling, in which the manufacturer retains control over the goods until they are sold, thus reducing the need for the distributor or dealer to use his own cash, and at the same time enabling him to maintain control over the price and over the terms and conditions of sale. This is like having one's own inventory stored in the dealer's or distributor's warehouse.

The final type of management strategy deals with decisions made by top management. This is called an *executive-based* strategy. It may include acquisitions, joint-venturing, consortiums, mergers, and management contracts, as well as self-development. For example, a company may decide to grow by acquiring other companies. This approach was used by many of the conglomerates in the 1960s. Joint developments have been successful in penetrating foreign markets and in creating new products that require more than one sophisticated technology. In some situations, the cost and capital needs have been so extensive that consortiums of specialists have been required to straighten them out.

Thus, there are a variety of ways to execute and lead an organization to achieve its financial and investment goals.

Functional Requirements: Implementation Strategy

After selecting an investment strategy and an appropriate management strategy, you must next formulate the critical functional programs that will enable you to successfully implement the chosen strategies and achieve the desired results.

This includes manufacturing, engineering, marketing, finance, and management. For instance, in order to enter a new national market you may be required to have a local plant that produces at least 50% of the product. This is a result of nationalism and of the desire of developing nations to become more self-sufficient. You may also need a sales and distribution system manned by local nationals or, at the very least, by Americans who understand local customs, business requirements, and possibly local language. It may also be necessary to accept local currency or even to barter with local businessmen. You may need individuals who understand the complexity of dealing with foreign governments and who are willing to take the time necessary to initiate, negotiate, and consummate a deal. I once heard a knowledgeable sales manager say that if you get an order in the Eastern European area after one trip, you most likely have obtained a bad deal. Large orders in that part of the world may take years to arrange.

Thus, implementation strategy requires a careful evaluation of what *must* be done to succeed. The success factors need to be complete and comprehensive. This evaluation must include all areas of the business, and it must be specific. Programs will attempt to outline how to use current strengths and how to correct limitations and resource deficiencies.

Some *engineering* strategies may require unique laboratories, special technological skills, and long and costly research, whereas others may demand the ability to translate concept and theory into practical applications. Other strategies may require special design abilities or engineers who are willing and able to follow or even copy existing models. Finally, there are strategies that require little or no technical skills; in fact, the very availability of those skills may hamper the proper execution of the strategy.

Having the wrong kind of sales force, distributors, or agents may be enough to invalidate a *marketing* strategy. Not providing sufficient service or inventory can also mean failure. Reliance on too little "market research" or the inability to design a product to fit the customer's requirements may also be disastrous. Implementation strategy requires a close examination of all marketing functions, including research, product planning, service, promotion, distribution, and pricing. *Financial* strategies should help you determine the nature and extent of your cash and capital requirements. If you need special billing, credit, or collections approaches, or if you will be dealing in foreign currencies that may fluctuate dramatically, then you may need to identify programs that cope with these problems. How and when bills are paid, and their terms of payment, may also be crucial. In addition, some strategies will require long-term financing, and you will need individuals who can negotiate the least expensive debt or equity financing. If a strategy aims at government markets, you will need individuals who can follow government accounting rules and regulations.

Management ability, perhaps the most vital of all, may cover special skills, backgrounds, or attitudes—even values may enter into the evaluation. Some managers are unable to respond quickly. Others are not suited to work in certain cultures. Still others cannot stand pressure, or cannot adapt to the relative stability of a strategy that calls for holding or gradually harvesting. There are many cases in which individuals who have a desire to innovate are asked to lead businesses that have a marketing thrust. This usually results in failure.

In the next two chapters, I shall describe some key elements of how a strategy is formulated and how you decide which strategy is most suitable to your environment, competitive climate, and resource strengths. But first, I would like to review why strategic planning is vital today and why it will continue to be vital in the future.

Why Is Strategic Planning Important?

Limited and Increasingly Expensive Resources

Only a decade ago most managers would have laughed if you had told them that oil, gas, and electricity would be limited to such an extent that the shortage of these resources would cause plants to be closed. Yet twice in the 1970s we have witnessed this very situation, and most knowledgeable observers warn that it will occur again and again. Today, financial resources are also limited. Only a few years ago, there was a capital crunch that also surprised many: Venture capital became practically unavailable, cash flows shrank, and interest rates soared. Capital and cash were actually scarce resources.

Because of the scarcity of money and resources most companies must become more selective and limit their investment to those businesses that can provide an attractive payoff and in which they are strong. Furthermore, they must count on some businesses to finance the growth of others. Thus, they need a resource allocation system that will enable them to select their best prospects. This is the purpose of strategic planning as described in this book.

Dynamic and Complex Changes

Every industry has been affected by the new requirements and demands of government and society. These have influenced how products are sold, and how they are manufactured. Laws have been passed which prohibit the sale of certain products, such as the ban on disposable beverage cans in Oregon. Other regulations prevent the use of certain kinds of ingredients, like aerosol gases, and still others require employers to hire certain kinds of people.

Extremely high rates of inflation and taxes have negatively affected earnings and the company's ability to update and replace equipment. All these forces have resulted in new market, customer, and industry conditions and have forced companies to rely less on "seat of the pants," opportunistic management. Contingencies have now become a reality, and a growing number of managers have indicated plans to deal with them—if they occur.

Increased Competition

Most American companies have experienced significant changes in their competitive climate. New competitors have entered established markets, often acquiring weak competitors and providing them with sufficient resources to make them much stronger. Competition from functional substitutes (such as the substitution of metal in cars with plastic) has become a reality, and has often caught companies unprepared. As a result, new competitors have changed the rules and the way the industry behaves. But competitive change isn't limited merely to new competitors; many of the existing competitors have applied strategic planning disciplines and have limited their scope, thus enabling them to be stronger in those businesses in which they have chosen to remain. This in turn has made strategic planning a vital need both for offensive and defensive purposes.

Whether we like it or not, strategic planning is here to stay, and it will become an increasingly important managerial skill for decades to come.

Designating Responsibilities

Strategic planning must permeate the entire organization. It requires analysis, synthesis, decision making, review, communication, and continual feedback. I have heard many people say that strategy development is the sole and nondelegatable responsibility of the chief executive officer. This is true if you believe that strategy is only investment strategy, but as I have shown, strategy has three levels, and each is crucial.

Top management, most often the chief executive officer and his close associates, makes the key decisions on investment strategy. It must decide which businesses will get heavy, moderate, few, or no investment dollars.

The next level of management, often the general managers of the various company divisions, is responsible for the selection of management strategy. These people are closest to their markets, customers, and competitors and, with the help of their own internal staffs, they can determine whether the leading thrust should be innovative, marketing, or manufacturing, or whether some entirely different approach should be taken.

The key functional managers—with the help of their bosses and the reviews of top-level staff—are responsible for the development of implementation strategies. Each functional manager must ensure that his programs are integrated into the strategy of the company as a whole.

But these decisions must be based on information analysis supplied by professionals throughout the organization, who must understand what is expected of them. Hence, relevant information must be disseminated to people who have decision-making responsibility. In the next two chapters, I shall describe what data are important and whether they are best supplied by operating personnel, internal staff, or outside consultants.

PART I

Strategic Thinking and Decisions

2

Highlights of
Strategic Thinking

BEFORE I discuss management strategy options, I shall briefly review the most critical aspects of strategic thinking and planning. A few years ago I wrote a book on strategic thinking in which I emphasized the various aspects of the process and how to integrate these stages to make strategic decisions. Since then, I have spent a considerable amount of time applying these concepts and processes, and have found certain aspects more critical than others. It is these areas that I would like to review with you. (If you would like a more complete review of the process, I'd recommend my earlier work.*)

* *Putting It All Together* (New York: AMACOM, 1976).

Strategic thinking requires four basic activities:

1. A clear understanding of where your company has been and why it has either succeeded or failed to achieve its expected results (both internal and external factors).
2. An identification of future trends or events that can change these results, either positively or negatively.
3. A review of current strategy at all three levels, a decision to change or not to change it, and a specification of the degree and type of change necessary.
4. The establishment of a system to monitor critical underlying decisions and a contingency plan to minimize impact.

Where Have You Been and How Successful Are You?

Psychologists tell us to "know thyself," and this is the first step in any sound strategic analysis as well. It sounds so easy and yet it is extremely difficult to clearly describe the kind of company you have. In addition, many executive officers assume that everyone sees the company as they themselves see it—this is a mistake that often has tragic consequences. In any strategic analysis, there are three characteristics that should be clearly articulated:

— What kind of markets have you participated in, and what has been the scope of your involvement? This may include consumer, industrial, domestic, or international markets, and you may specify your involvement as being that of a generalist or a specialist.
— What has been your product position and type? Have you been considered an innovator or leader? Have you provided components, materials, or total systems?
— What has been your economic position? This could include your profitability, debt position, and financial leverage.

This should be completed for all *key segments* of your total corporation, especially if your company is diversified. Here are a few examples of how you might use these questions to describe your company.

IBM could be described as a company dedicated to data processing equipment that serves all end-use markets on a worldwide basis. It has been a full-line producer, considered to be highly service-oriented with the ability to respond quickly to technical innovation, although IBM itself does not normally introduce innovations. Its financial position and performance are second to none. It has excellent liquidity, estimated in the $7 billion range, and no long-term debt.

McDonald's could be described as a specialist that services the fast-food consumer market but that has been able to differentiate itself through creative merchandising and franchising, primarily in the United States, but also in other developed Americanized countries. Its financial performance is highest among similar companies, and it doubles the industry median with a 26.3% return on equity, a 9.5% return on sales, and an earnings-per-share growth of 33.5%.

Therefore, you can see that in a few sentences a company can describe its product, market, and financial direction and position, but it is more difficult for insiders who have too much knowledge than it would be for the more objective outside observer.

Why Have You Achieved Your Present Status?

The next question requires even more insight and objectivity: Why has the company achieved its current stature and financial performance? The explanation must be viewed in two ways. First, what external forces have contributed to this success or failure? Second, what competitive leverage has contributed to these results?

External Factors

Environment has several dimensions. There is the immediate, or so-called microenvironment, and there is the larger universe, called the macroenvironment. Both need to be examined. I shall pay particular attention to those key factors that most often determine the success or failure of an enterprise.

Macroenvironmental events, factors, and trends can either enhance or hinder the prospect of success. Normally these factors affect the market, the customer, the competition, or the company's own resources. These conditions should also be described in any strategic analysis of your firm, so that changes on this level can be anticipated.

Suppose you were doing business in the 1950s. How would you have summarized the macroenvironment?

Economy Growing rapidly; inflation under control; high level of consumer confidence.

Society Relatively complacent. The big issues were Korea and McCarthyism, but these didn't have a great effect on consumer behavior or confidence.

Technology Electronics, materials, and data processing were in their infancy; they were used for military and experimental purposes and were written about in science fiction books.

Political The Eisenhower Era—little public involvement in politics.

The total effect of all these external factors to the business strategist was minimal. It was business as usual, with little concern about tomorrow. It was easy to be complacent and not wonder about change.

In the 1960s, the environment was almost the exact opposite to that of the 1950s, and the macroenvironment had a much greater impact on business, although the full consequences of the events of that decade weren't felt until the early 1970s. The point should be obvious: Macroenvironmental events do affect the business climate and eventually have an impact on the conduct of individual firms as well.

Market Factors

Understanding where the product or segment is in the life cycle of the *market* is another important consideration. You may have succeeded because you were in the early or rapid-growth stage, which permitted you to be less than efficient and still achieve remarkable growth in sales and income. Furthermore, customers may have been eager to pay premiums due to either their desire to buy or a scarcity of supply, or both. In addition, you may have had predecessors who had excellent personal relationships with the customer's key decision makers, or who provided flexible, low-interest terms and conditions of payments. These individuals may have had foresight or the willingness to assume risks. Thus, they added capacity in advance of demand and thereby provided you with the leverage and readiness to serve. Certainly the current management of IBM has a lot to thank its predecessors for—especially Thomas Watson, Sr.—and before it takes credit for the company's current strong market position, it must take into consideration the contributions of its predecessors.

There are other areas to examine—for instance, the nature of distribution and user dealers, because again your position with the distributor may help account for the success you now have.

Evaluating your *customers* from a strategic perspective is another key ingredient in strategic planning, and may help develop the insights you require. For instance, did your customer have unique needs that you and your product were able to meet? Was he growing rapidly and did he have unique financial strengths? Did you have the ability to guide him in selecting and using your product effectively? Was he selective or indiscriminate in seeking sales and volume growth? All of these questions could account for the growth and success you have had and, as I will explain in the next section, may be factors that will change in the future, thereby requiring new strategic thrusts on your part. In essence, we must understand how the customer's objectives, goals, and strategies dovetailed with yours.

Industry Factors

Questions about service, pricing, capacity, warranties, and competitors' behavior in the particular industry can also give insight into why a company did well or poorly financially. Service may have been a big concern of the customer at all stages of the product life. I just mentioned pre-sales and applications services that may have been vital to a customer because he had no experience, didn't know what he wanted, and his staff was unskilled in the matters at hand. Or he may have been concerned about repair or maintenance or the availability of spare and replacement parts. All of these may have resulted in the customer's paying a little more and selecting you as his vendor. Prices may have been high because of these factors or because competitors all priced highly and refused to compete on the basis of price alone.

Capacity may have had a high-profitability level, and competitors may have refused to reduce prices just to fill the plant. Warranties and guarantees may have favored the supplier, not the users, and the competitors may have been well known and highly homogeneous, each seeking similar objectives. There have been many examples of industries like these in all sectors of the economy. At times their actions have been due purely to statesmanlike behavior, and at other times they were a result of arrangements among cartels or trusts. Today we are witnessing the best example of this behavior— the Organization of Petroleum Exporting Countries (OPEC). Again, the point is to understand your environment so that you can anticipate change and then determine how to respond.

How much of a company's past success can be accounted for by a unique *technological* position, based on either product or process? There are many successful companies whose only reason for success was their unique patents or in-plant skills and know-how. It is also important to understand why a particular technology was viewed so fondly by the customer. This also requires insight into the competing technology and why it wasn't received as well.

Thus, your current position and industry attractiveness may have been a result of one or more of these key factors. The really big winners seem to have had rapid growth in their markets and customers who were enamored of their products and who were willing to pay a premium to get to use them. Furthermore, the industry was inhabited by businessmen who understood how to keep competitive conditions on a nonprice plan and who were cautious about building too much capacity or offering unrealistic warranties or financial terms. Finally, the successful companies were ranked highly and had some product, technical, production, market, or financial leverage to be winners. They weren't merely lucky—it takes management and executive skill to be a *perennial* winner—but they had an attractive environment and a strong position, and invested to capitalize on it. Often the big losers lacked one or several parts of this equation: The markets collapsed, or the customers became more cautious or price-conscious, or the competitors began to act greedily or foolishly, or the companies themselves lacked the power to act decisively—on occasion, their management proved completely inept.

Anticipating Change or Lack of Change

The next step in sound strategic thinking and planning involves looking forward, both at what you would like to be and at how the environment and resources are likely to change. Although the question of change in product, market, or financial scope is preliminary at this stage, it is worth raising. Essentially you are asking whether you are satisfied with the company you manage. For example, do you wish to concentrate on your current markets or industries, or would you like to look to greener pastures or to become more specialized? Are you content with your current image or leadership? Would you like to move either closer to your user customers or farther from them? How about the results you have been able to achieve—are they sufficient? These can help you in determining how complex the planning exercise will be. The diagram in Figure 2–1 may help. Again, you should

Figure 2-1. Expansion and reduction of the market scope of two businesses.

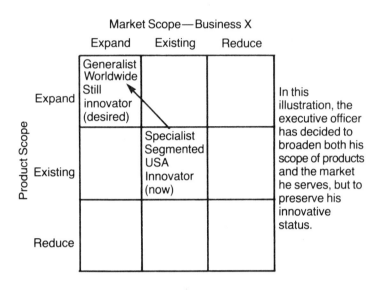

Market Scope—Business X

In this illustration, the executive officer has decided to broaden both his scope of products and the market he serves, but to preserve his innovative status.

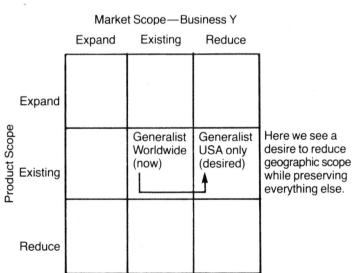

Market Scope—Business Y

Here we see a desire to reduce geographic scope while preserving everything else.

use one of the diagrams for *each* business and the corporation as a whole.

Whether you can successfully make these moves and achieve the results you desire can't be effectively determined unless you examine and anticipate the future environment. This requires several types of analyses:

1. You should examine those market, customer, industry, and other characteristics, as well as those of your own abilities, that have contributed to your past successes and failures; then, you can identify what may change.

2. You should look more broadly at the environment and future resources related to any anticipated moves, especially if you are moving into markets or industries beyond your experiential base.

3. Examine all other micro- and macroenvironmental conditions that can make tomorrow's world different.

Next, I'd like to review some conditions that I have found can really make a difference in all three of these analytical steps.

Conditions That Affect Change

The Customer

First, we must never lose sight of the *customer* and how changes in his objectives, needs, and decision making can affect our business. Customers change and mature, and this will make an impact on your business, whether they use your product or not. For instance, the demographic changes in the United States population can have a dynamic impact on consumer products.

The February 1977 issue of *Dun's Review*—as well as many other business, governmental, and academic journals—pointed out that Americans are growing older, will have smaller families, will be more affluent, will have new sex roles, and thus will have different needs and wants in the future. This could rapidly enhance the growth of some products and cause others to decline more rapidly. Is the fascination with "youth" and "symbols of youth" over? Or will this trend continue in the future? Or will it be a cyclical occurrence?

Consumer customers aren't the only ones who change; so do *industrial customers.* Sometimes they change their priorities: Witness Illinois Central's move to deemphasize railroads and move more aggressively into consumer products (i.e., recreational vehicles) and automotive replacement parts (Midas). This strategic change could be significant to you if you sold locomotives or refurbished railroad cars, since the Illinois Central Corporation may stop investing in these products and put the earnings generated by its railroad assets into a new muffler plant.

This illustrates another important economic change— namely, the impact of *acquisitions* and *mergers.* If you had sold to Midas when it was a separate company, your sales may have been small or may have grown slowly, since Midas didn't have sufficient investment funds for rapid expansion. But witness what happened when Midas was acquired by Illinois Central Railroad: It expanded more rapidly and you as a supplier may have been unprepared. The same condition is apparent in the oil industry. Mobil is moving aggressively into the consumer arena with its acquisition of Marcor Inc. (the result of a previous merger between Container Corporation of America and Montgomery Ward).

Diversification moves change priorities and can influence market growth. Governmental and regulated customers can also change. Their needs may move from building facilities, paving roads, and adding sewerage to administering social programs (such as welfare, unemployment, and day care). Their ability to finance and fund these projects and the ratio of fixed to discretionary funds in their budgets will also change. For instance, an increasing percentage of tax money in New York City is going into pension liabilities and payment of past debts, and thus may not be available for spending on your products. Of course, the decision-making procedures also change, and so do the decision makers. Decisions may be slowed down because of a change in office holders, or they may be accelerated because the budget has extra money that must be spent before the end of the fiscal year. The point to be kept in mind is that customers do change, thus causing changes in market size, growth rates, and the nature of the products they require. Tracking the customer and assessing market impact and the changes in where the product is in the life cycle is the responsibility of the marketing and planning organizations. This requires more than just a sales orientation; it means that the marketing staff must try to understand the customers' strategies and resource situations. This includes studying their annual reports, reviewing their press releases and speeches, and evaluating their financial statements. Periodic meetings with their senior executives and planning staff may help you determine if they contemplate a strategic change that can affect their products and sales.

Changes in the Competitive Situation

Another area in which change can have a major impact is that of competition. As we all know, competition comes in many shapes and forms. First, there are the existing competitors who offer similar, though possibly differentiated, products. These competitors can change if their management changes or if they are acquired by another company. New management may change the strategy from a holding to an aggressive growth strategy, and you may be the target.

Mergers and acquisitions can also change the nature of the competitive situation, by bringing new resources to competitors. For example, Raytheon's acquisition of Amana permitted Amana to become a stronger, more aggressive appliance manufacturer, since Amana's own strong marketing and manufacturing skills were complemented by Raytheon's financial and technological strengths. Of course, both management and ownership changes can weaken a competitor or make it less competent. There are hundreds of instances in which the founder of a business retired or died and his successor lacked the skills to lead effectively. If you are competing against ITT or IBM or Ford, you must carefully evaluate the loss of the founding fathers or the dominant leaders to determine the impact of such an event. Certainly, RCA has never been the same since the retirement and subsequent death of General David Sarnoff.

Another change that should be anticipated is the entry of a competitor from another segment of the business, either by direct entry or by merger or acquisition. Recently, American companies have had a difficult time competing with their Japanese and European counterparts. This, I believe, has occurred for a variety of reasons; primarily because American companies didn't understand the nature of their own markets and industries. They lulled themselves into a false sense of security by not understanding why customers bought their products, and they often underestimated their ability to hold share at higher prices or at less attractive terms. They believed that the need for extensive distribution or service networks couldn't be duplicated or that the foreign competitors' products were of lower quality or didn't meet the needs of consumers. They misread or totally ignored the foreign companies' resources, objectives, and commitment. For example, most American companies still aren't aware that foreign companies have interlocking directorships, intimate ties with their own governments, and the ability to reduce reported earnings via accrual accounting and favorable tax laws, and that foreign companies are willing to suffer initial losses for future gains. Understanding this requires a management team which can put itself into its competitor's shoes and ask objectively, "If I were him, what would I do?"

But geographic segment moves aren't the only kind. There are illustrations of a "low-price" competitor deciding to move into the middle- and high-price segment. For example, Texas Instruments has moved from the low and middle segment of the calculator market into the higher, more sophisticated end, thus becoming a threat to Hewlett-Packard. Sears has attempted to upgrade its line, with mixed success so far. So have the department store chains, which have moved into discounting, catalogue stores, specialty shops, and so on. Dayton-Hudson Properties, a midwestern department store chain which started as a traditional department store, has opened up and acquired a number of specialty shops, including B. Dalton Bookseller, Team Central, Inc., Lechmere Tire & Sales and Target Discount Stores, and four jewelry stores.

The point is that you must not assume that a particular firm won't move from one segment to another.

Changes Caused by Introduction of New Technology

In any attempt to secure a competitive edge by introducing a new technology, one very serious strategic flaw is to forget what the customer wants and to become preoccupied with the means you use to satisfy this want. You must always ask, "What is the function or need the customer wishes to satisfy, and how can this need be met?" For instance, consumers want transportation that is convenient and less costly, and they can meet this need in a variety of ways—public transportation, for one. This was graphically demonstrated when Westport, Connecticut, initiated its Mini-Bus service. The city offered convenient, low-cost, deluxe buses in a highly status-conscious community, and it worked. Many people sold their "station wagon or second car," and took the bus to the train station. In 1977, the city introduced another service, "Maxi-Taxi," which provided taxi service at lower cost. Transportation can be provided by automobiles, trains, taxis, bikes, small scooters, motorcycles, and so on. Consumers may choose any or all of these, without caring whether the vehicle is gasoline-, electricity-, steam-, or solar-powered, provided that it meets their functional and economic needs.

What's the lesson? Try to anticipate what the consumers or users will do. Empathize with them. Ask what they really want and how it can be provided. Study the options objectively, and evaluate them periodically. Don't become locked in; don't become arrogant or defensive. There may be a better way to do what you've been doing—there are illustrations of technological substitutions in all industries:

Housing Aluminum and vinyl siding for wood
Cars Diesel-powered for gas-powered, and in the future, a
  strong possibility of electrically-powered cars.
Controls Electronic for electro-mechanical
Power Nuclear for fossil fuel (i.e., coal, oil) and in the
  future, solar.

In each case, the new technology brings in a host of new competitors who will, predictably, think, plan, and behave differently.

Changes in the Distribution Network

Changes in how the customer obtains his product (the distribution network) are becoming more and more important. Many customers become so experienced with the product and buy it in such quantities that they want to bypass the intermediary and buy direct. The "I can get it wholesale" mentality has led to the growth of volume retail outlets, often called discounters. This has had dramatic impact on the entire retail structure, and those companies that relied on small, independent retailers (sometimes called "mom and pop" stores, since they were run by husband-and-wife teams) were forced either to change their sales, pricing, and promotional programs or to be content with a declining share of the market. These changes continue to take place and have become more confused since the traditional department stores have moved into discounting. The result has often been disruption of traditional segmentation schemes. Furthermore, the small independents have pooled their resources to purchase in quantity, thereby permitting them to compete effectively with the major retail chains. This, too, has caused the growth of new wholesale distributors.

But this pattern of change hasn't been limited to the consumer markets alone. In industrial markets, large customers have set up mechanisms to buy direct and in quantity, thus forcing the manufacturers to establish direct sales approaches. Furthermore, industrial customers have become more experienced, and have cut down on their need to pay for services. They have been willing to accept fewer guarantees and warranties, or have become so powerful that they can demand service and warranties at no extra cost.

Changes in the Governmental Sector

The governmental sector has also changed, and this has forced companies to reexamine their sales and pricing practices. Municipal governments have become stronger and, because of legal requirements, have forced manufacturers and service companies to sell on the basis of sealed bids. The complexity of selling offshore to governmental and quasi-governmental customers has increased, and the problem shows no signs of letting up; in fact, most believe it will get worse. Thus the entire area of industry characteristics and approaches to the marketplace has become an area of significant change.

Changes in the Supply of Resources

Yet another area worthy of critical evaluation is supply. What will happen to the supply of your materials, components, and services in the coming years? How will this affect your ability to compete? Many companies have had success because of the availability of minerals that cost little and were easy to obtain. In fact, Americans now realize that low-cost energy, in the form of oil or natural gas, provided them with a unique competitive advantage that everybody took for granted. This became a startling revelation in the early 1970s. Now, everyone must carefully examine supply and key suppliers. For example, how plentiful and how available will the supply be? Who are the key suppliers and what is their strategy? Will the number of suppliers decline, possibly forcing a single or sole-source situation? A supplier may decide to discontinue a component that is critical to you simply because it doesn't fit into its business strategy of because its continued production is unprofitable to the supplier. Or a supplier may be acquired or merged into another company, possibly a competitor, thereby putting your fate in the hands of a competitor. Or a nation may decide to nationalize all its national resource producers because of political rather than economic reasons, and thereby limit or cut off your access to that resource.

For example, many Americans take our steel, aluminum, chrome, and platinum products for granted, but they don't realize that availability of many of these metals depends on supply sources in Rhodesia and South Africa. No one can sympathize with the racial practices of these nations, but it could be a major setback to American industrial growth and prosperity if these countries were to fall into the hands of Communist powers. Some analysts believe that controlling these nations and the Mideast is part of the worldwide strategy of the Soviet Union. If the Russians were to succeed in dominating this area, then their power would be greater than that of all the nuclear weapons in their arsenal. Under these circumstances, even if Russia didn't cut the supply lines, it could cause economic chaos at will.

Consider what would happen to your costs and your ability to complete and to make a profit if there was a scarcity of minerals and oil. Today, there are some products that are made by only one or two producers. Could you remain in business if you had only one supplier? The message is clear: Anticipate a change in the supply situation!

Changes in Finance and in the Workforce

The availability and cost of money can significantly affect any business. Again, remember the credit crunch of the 1970s. What would you do if interest rates were to reach 25% again and you have long-term debt maturing or have relied heavily on short-term debt? And what if capital weren't available at any price? (Some economists say that this is impossible, that capital will always be available if you are willing to pay for it.) Would you be prepared to cope with such contingencies if they were to arise?

The nature and productivity of your total workforce should also be evaluated. Again, there are many social and political trends that could affect your organizational response. The forced entry of less skilled individuals could add cost, reduce quality, and weaken your position. Workers' drive for more time off, automatic salary increases, and excessive benefits can reduce productivity. The desire to retire earlier, or the concept of "portable" pensions (i.e., the pension liability transfers with the individual to his new employer), could increase pension liabilities and reduce earnings available for

Figure 2-2. Sources of change that affect your market.

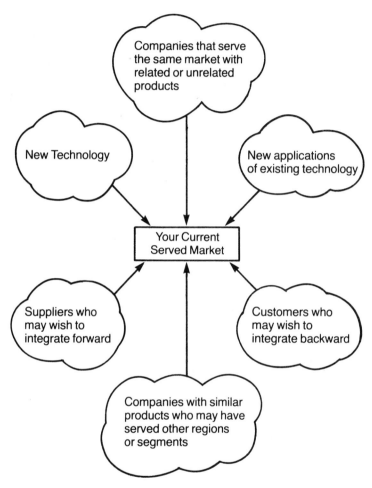

reinvestment in the business. The refusal of employees to transfer and move can alter the flexibility of your workforce.

Thus, as you can see in Figure 2–2, all areas are undergoing change and each can seriously affect the factors that have contributed to your success in the past.

Sources of Information for Strategic Analysis

In formulating a strategic analysis, you are trying to describe where you have been and where the future may take you if you continue to do what you have been doing. There are five basic sources of information about your environment and your relative position: your own operating managers and their professionals, corporate staff officers and specialists, outside consultants, associations, and the government. These sources can help evaluate the factors that have contributed to your company's success or failure and how these factors may change in the future, either positively or negatively.

Operating Managers and Professionals

Operating managers and professionals should be required to explain why they think they have succeeded or failed and to state what they believe will contribute to their future success. Operating managers are the closest to their markets, customers, industry, and technology. Their marketing staff should be questioned about the market size, growth, and cyclicality, as well as about customer strategy and buying behavior. The staff should be asked to anticipate changes in the industry, especially those pertaining to service or to applications of new or existing technology. In conjunction with finance, you should inquire about pricing, terms, conditions, and profitability. Financial managers are the record keepers and the custodians of historical market and profit data, but they must be urged to analyze the financial data from a market and external perspective so that the data will be of use in formulating strategies. Quite often, finance will only analyze investor and tax requirements but not in a manner that will enable management to explain the market.

Manufacturing and engineering departments must also play a role. For instance, manufacturing and engineering organizations maintain a relationship with the customer after the sale has been made. This may take the form of helping the customer learn how to use and apply the equipment, repairing the equipment if it doesn't work, maintaining it, or just providing spare parts. The engineering staff may learn that the customer has plans to move his manufacturing facilities, or to open a new one, or that he is experimenting with new processes, materials, or technologies that may open up new opportunities or create new threats to the company. Through complaints and failures, the manufacturing and technical staff can learn about what the customer expects or requires in the future. Finally, the engineering and research staff must be aware of its responsibilities to technological and competitive trends both inside and outside its immediate market and industry. This is like an early warning system that will alert the company to new technical trends and events and that will enable it to make alternative and contingency responses.

Thus, one of the best sources of anticipating changes and explaining past results is your own operating people. They must recognize this responsibility and must be rewarded or punished depending on their effectiveness in carrying out this task. This is particularly important since operating people normally don't think that they have a real role, and the normal corporate reward system confirms this belief by only rewarding them for operating results.

The Corporate Staff

But even with a system of rewards and punishments, comprehensive strategic analysis will require data to be converted systematically into intelligence and then evaluated for its strategic relevance and importance. This requires the discipline and involvement of a competent, objective, and demanding staff. A good staff is vital to planning and, whether it be large or small, it must be disciplined and thorough. Staffers must ask the tough and even seemingly sacrilegious questions in an attempt to find out what is fact and what is merely gossip. There is a mythology which develops around all businesses. Staffers must constantly ask, Why? What is the source of this rumor? They should avoid being lulled into a false sense of security while resisting the temptation of only seeing the dark side. Staffers should be the devil's advocates, but they should not merely enjoy being critical and negative. The staff's job, then, is to systematically obtain, probe, validate, and embellish the internally generated data about the market, customers, industry, technology, and macroenvironmental forces. But even the best internal staff, regardless of its size, can't be expected to do the total job. First, it will have a difficult time remaining objective. Once its advice is either accepted or rejected, it will become part of the problem and will be unable to develop alternative approaches. Second, the universe is just too large and complex for any internal staff to follow and understand. Thus, there is a need for the third source of data: External professional consultants. (Incidentally, a good staff should know when it needs help from outsiders, and it should be able to assist outside consultants in doing their jobs as well.)

Outside Consultants

Consulting help comes in a wide variety of shapes and forms. There are one-man operations, which guide executives in their decision making—this is called personal consulting. There are also large numbers of smaller consulting firms, which specialize in specific industries, do special studies, evaluate current practices, and provide thinking. Then there are academicians who freelance or work in conjunction with their universities. Finally, there are the large consulting operations, like McKinsey, Arthur D. Little, Booz Allen & Hamilton, Stanford Research Institute (SRI), and so on. I shall focus on this type, not because it is superior to the small independent but because it provides a large number of services that you should know about.

Essentially there isn't one "best" consultant; that will depend on the problem you have and on how quickly you would like it to be solved. If you have a single problem or wish to study one specific industry, or competitor, then the small independent may be most appropriate. If, however, you have a critical problem or wish to study the whole company and all its segments, and if time is crucial, then the larger and more prestigious organizations will be best for you. At times, it is important just to have the blessing of someone or some organization that has a strong reputation.

A consultant or consulting firm is basically selling experience and special skills. A number of firms sell prepackaged, off-the-shelf studies and services, which may be about specific industries, emerging markets, trends, procedures, and approaches. I would like to examine some of these firms now.

Stanford Research Institute of Menlo Park, California, provides a long-range planning service and has hundreds of reports for sale. This service began in 1958, and is one of the oldest of its kind. In 1958 it issued three reports, two on emerging new products and markets (synthetic fibers and irradiated foods) and the third on the European Common Market. In 1959 it issued 30 reports, of which many are still interesting today. These include studies of the prefabricated housing market, of the availability of new sources of electric energy, and of business communications systems. These and other reports have been periodically updated and supplemented. In addition to its research reports, SRI provides briefs, special studies, and guidelines. Some of its publications deal with planning and organization, such as the role of the corporate planner, the planning organization, the diversification plan, the long-range plan, and the operating plan.

Several organizations have been formed by individuals who left SRI and created their own companies. One of these is Creative Strategies, Inc., located in Palo Alto, California. Creative Strategies concentrates on new, high-technology-based industries and markets. I have studied a number of reports written by Creative Strategies and I was impressed by their quality. The reports included studies of computer input and output, health care, instrumentation, office equipment, pollution control, semiconductors, small computers, and telecommunications. It has even done studies of specific companies, like Sony. The outline of the reports includes all the topics I have discussed in this book. For instance, one report included a discussion of the market, industry, technology, and competition, as well as the success factors they believe to be critical in the microwave oven business.

Arthur D. Little's Impact Services is another useful service. It tries to develop an understanding of business environments and of the resources it takes to succeed. Since 1972, ADL has issued reports on every conceivable industry, including fibers, aerosols, antibiotics, building components and materials, business communications, cable television, clinical laboratory diagnostics, and energy. These reports are continually updated and supplemented to keep them current.

The reports sold by Frost and Sullivan have also provided assistance in several strategies I have developed. This firm has reports covering the chemical industry, communications, electronics, consumer data processing, energy, financial and business services, and health care, among others.

As I said, I have used all of these services, as well as others, including those provided by industry associations, universities, stock and investment analysts, banks, trade publications, and The Conference Board. These have been beneficial in giving me strategic insights and in helping me develop some of the alternatives I will describe later. But they are only part of the analysis and synthesis required to do the job that I believe is necessary. In all cases, they have given me different opinions or insights and have assured me that I wouldn't become myopic or provincial. Furthermore, I have used conflicts and varying opinions as a means of determining what I wish to study further, which has often led to my retaining the services of another consultant or organization to do specific and more direct studies.

All the firms I have mentioned provide customized and proprietary studies. For a fee, they will provide access to their own files or they will probe further to get additional information. McKinsey and Boston Consulting specialize in studies across the strategic planning spectrum. These firms will study your own resources to determine your relative position in the market, and in addition, will recommend alternative strategies and plans.

These proprietary studies, when combined with packaged studies, and the opinions and analyses of your own operating staff, are invaluable to the development of strategic alternatives. But here are a few words of caution: You must know what you expect the consultant to accomplish and how his findings will fit into the total picture, then you must properly plan and manage the consultants. They must be challenged and asked the same tough questions that I recommend you ask your operating and staff personnel. Consultants are only human, and they use much of the same information you use yourself. Quite often, they will base their conclusions and recommendations on their intuition and experience. This is fine, but you must still differentiate fact from opinion.

Another point to remember is that, like anyone else, consultants vary in skill and ability. Know which individual will be working on your project and what role the senior consultant or partner will play. Most often the senior members of the firm will do the presentation before and after the study, but will have little involvement in the study itself. You should demand that they help generate alternatives or evaluate the viability of the final decision. However, it isn't realistic or even economically sound to have the senior members do the data collection and analysis; that is the work of the junior consultants.

There is nothing wrong in using the services of a variety of consultants, but this is a very complicated procedure and must be planned carefully to obtain the most value and to prevent unnecessary conflict among the consultant, your staff, and internal operating managers. Sometimes too many opinions confuse rather than help the situation.

Other Sources of Information

I mentioned that outside associations, institutions, and the government have also proved to be inexpensive and helpful. Because they are more generic and less costly, their reports often require more interpretation than those of consultants.

Every industry has a *trade or industry association* that collects and distributes raw data about market size; growth; price and cost trends; new product opportunities; and new trends in distribution, advertising, and manufacturing processes and equipment. Most often, these associations have a limited staff and provide little interpretation of their data. This is to be expected because all competitors have equal access to the information, and the organization must avoid being involved in illegal antitrust activities. (This is not the case in foreign countries where the trade association is often the equivalent of a cartel.) I have found that participation in these associations can be helpful if you recognize their deficiencies and are willing to supplement their services. This is particularly true if the association has a Washington office that keeps up with legislation that could directly or indirectly affect the industry and its members.

Most of the major *stock and investment firms* provide reports about the industries and companies they follow. The individuals assigned to cover these industries often provide interesting insights into what is going on and what may affect the profitability and growth of the markets. These services put out extremely comprehensive reports on particular industries, and often their reports duplicate the studies that are prepared by the consulting houses. Again, you must recognize the limitations of these firms' reports: Investors are interested in the short-term prospects of the company and the industry, not its long-range outlook, so these reports may ignore environmental trends that might affect the long-range future. Also, many analysts evaluate only the financial records of a company, and fail to understand *why* those results have been achieved.

University business schools produce thousands of case studies and these can be used in the study both of companies and of total industries. The more detailed case studies have industry notes that provide background about the industry and its past. They don't provide forecasts, but these can be obtained from other sources. You can get a listing of all the case studies and the industry notes by writing to the Intercollegiate Case Clearing House at Harvard University, Boston, Massachusetts.

Banks and lending institutions provide services similar to those offered by stock and brokerage firms. Often these institutions have compiled a thorough analysis of past developments, and even have econometric models to forecast future trends and results in various industries. These services can be purchased from the lending institutions themselves.

In every issue of the *popular business magazines—Business Week, Dun's Review, Fortune, Forbes,* and *The Wall Street Journal*—there are articles about specific companies, markets, new products, and governmental actions. These articles provide another point of view about the industry or subject being discussed. You may be able to find out more by getting in touch with the magazine or by attending one of the seminars they offer to the public. Again, remember that all sources have their limitations. At times, the articles in these magazines are based purely on hearsay, and lack the depth of research that you may require. Furthermore, their stories may be based on the sources I have already mentioned. I have often found the same story repeated over and over again in these magazines without ever being challenged.

The U.S. Government Printing Office is the world's largest publisher and puts out thousands of *governmental publications* every year. These include reprints of congressional proceedings, speeches, findings of government-sponsored research, how-to publications, and reports on all countries of the world. The main problem with this source of information is that there is so much data you can get lost. Therefore, you must have a system, know exactly what you want, and then assign someone to obtain and interpret the information. Selectivity is vital.

In conclusion, strategic thinking and planning require a sound, objective, and critical evaluation of the past and the present as a foundation for predicting the future, as well as the kind of complex, multifactorial approach outlined in Table 2–1. If you lack insights into the reasons for your successes and failures, your future projections will also be misguided. In the later chapters of this book, I outline various options, but these must fit your resources and the environment in which you operate. Be careful not to commit yourself to a strategy that appears challenging and exciting but doesn't fit the needs of your business.

Table 2-1. Constructing a complete strategic analysis.

The Environment to Be Studied	Your Operating Managers	Your Staff	Outside Consultants	Other Associations	The Government
Market Growth Cyclicality Sensitivity Tie to macro-environment Your position	Marketing key—use their experience, intuition, judgment, information	Staff should use data provided and analyze them, as well as lead additional studies	Packaged reports Special studies	Trade associations Stock analysts Universities Banks Press Special seminars The Conference Board	Department of Commerce Special reports Antitrust reports Council of Economic Advisors
Customers Demographics Strategies Requirements Your position	Marketing/manufacturing	Special studies Special analyses	Special studies when there are packaged studies of specific companies	Stock analyses Rating institutions Special press reports Features in press	Special reports Antitrust cases Department of Commerce

Industry

Service	Marketing	Special studies	Special studies	Trade associations	Special reports
Pricing	Marketing/finance	Monitoring/trends analysis		Press	Department of Commerce
Capacity	Manufacturing			Special reports	Department of Justice
Terms				Seminars	Special publications
Conditions					
Profitability					
Guarantees					
Your position					

Technology

Patents	Legal	Special studies	Packaged reports	Technical societies	Department of Commerce
Research	Engineering	Special analyses	Special studies	University research	Department of Labor
Funding	Marketing			Special reports	Office of Technology
Applications	Engineering			Trade associations	Department of Defense
Process	Manufacturing			Special seminars	Patent Office
				Vendor/supplier publications	Special reports
					Research briefs

3

Making Decisions and Setting Priorities

THUS far I have outlined the key ingredients in strategic analysis, a task that can be either very extensive or merely an update of what you already know. The depth of analysis required is a function of what has been done in evaluating data in the past and of how much change you anticipate. I personally have spent several man-months evaluating the market, studying competitors, and assessing abilities. But the collection, documentation, and evaluation of data is a means, not an end, of strategic thinking. The end is making critical decisions. As I discussed in the first chapter, the first decision focuses on priorities and the allocation of financial and human resources. Where to invest; how much to invest; and why to invest—these are the issues addressed by Investment Strategy.

How to Set Investment Priorities

Using Rate of Return as a Criterion

The most simplistic approach to making this decision is to merely select those businesses or segments that have the highest financial return. Of course, there are several ways of doing this—you may choose to invest only in those areas that yield a high rate of return on investment, on sales, on net assets employed, and so on. This is commonly referred to as a "hurdle rate"—that is, if you can't make the minimum rate, you won't invest any more and may even withdraw or liquidate the investment you have already made. Obviously the height of the hurdle is critical: If the rate of return is too high, it may eliminate some very attractive situations; if it is too low, it doesn't help you differentiate good from poor investments, because too many industries pass through the screen. Most managers argue that the minimum acceptable rate is the "cost of money"—that is, the true interest rate. For instance, if it cost you 15% to borrow money, then you must be able to get at least a 15% return. It sounds logical and is very specific, but it has some problems. First of all, hurdle rates are very arbitrary but, more importantly, they are based on past, not future, returns and, as we all know, the past may not be replicated in the future. Finally, these rates may not be achievable in a given industry. I must therefore conclude that this is a unidimensional "management-by-objectives" approach.

Here is an illustration of how you can use hurdle rates to screen opportunities. Suppose you decide to diversify and that you have very firm ideas about the amount of returns you expect. Let us assume that you are seeking industries that have an average return on stockholder equity of 15% a year, and a return on total capital of at least 10%. In this case you can use the *Forbes* analyses published in the January edition each year. If you used the list for 1977 given in Table 3–1, you would find several industries that meet these two criteria.

Table 3–1. Rates of return on equity and on total capital in various industries.

Industry	*ROE* (Return on Equity) *Average (5 years)*	*ROTC (Return on Total Capital)* * *Average (5 years)*
Toiletries/cosmetics	19.8%	16.3%
Housekeeping products	16.8	13.5
Ethical drugs	22.4	20.0
Proprietary drugs	17.4	12.4
Oil and gas	15.7	11.1
Coal	23.5	17.0
Specialty chemicals	15.7	9.9
Food distributors	15.2	11.8
Agricultural commodities	16.1	11.4
Food specialists	15.0	10.5
Drinks	15.5	11.5
Electrical equipment	18.5	13.5
Mining/drilling equipment	15.1	13.1
Drug chains	15.0	12.7
Building equipment	17.4	15.6
Diversified metals	18.2	12.1
Truckers	24.3	13.1

* Return on Total Capital includes stockholders' equity plus capital from long-term debt, minority stockholders' equity, accumulated deferred taxes, and investment tax credit.

Using Growth as a Criterion

A second way of setting investment priorities is to look at businesses that have high growth, whether real or potential. In this case the rationale emphasizes the market, with the inference that growth is good and that profitability will inevitably follow. Again, we must first determine what is growth and what level is truly critical. Boston Consulting uses this as one critical measure, and has selected a 10% growth level as a hurdle growth rate.

Again using *Forbes,* you can formulate a list of industries that are growing most rapidly. Suppose you used a 15% per year compound growth as a cut-off point. Table 3–2 shows the industry list that you would compile.

Table 3-2. Average growth rates in various industries.

Industry	*Growth Average * (5 years)*
Heavy construction	15.8%
Home building	19.7
International oils	18.1
Other oil and gas	23.6
Coal	19.7
Food distribution	15.0
Agricultural commodities	17.2
Travel	21.5
Mining and drilling	17.1
Banking	20.4
Drug chains	20.2
Lumber	16.7
Truckers	17.7

* If Return on Equity is used as a measure; if Return on Total Capital is used, fewer industries show such high levels of growth.

Thus, you can see that the ratios you select and the level you use as a hurdle will affect the number of opportunities you will consider.

Like the approach based on rate of return, this method has the advantage of being specific and the disadvantage of being historical rather than future-based. But is also has one additional impediment—namely, that growth is equated to profitability. This is quite often not true: Growth markets are likely to be unprofitable in the early stages, and only the long-term survivors will make money.

This can be shown by comparing the data on ROE, ROTC, and growth rates. If you used the 15% ROE, 10% ROTC, and 15% annual growth rates as criteria, you would find that heavy construction, oil and gas, coal, food distribution, agricultural commodities, mining and drilling equipment, drug chains, and truckers pass the test, because they have high growth rates and high returns. But others, like home building, although growing rapidly (19.7%/yr), had a

9.2% return on equity and a 5.6% return on total capital. Travel grew at 21.5%, but returned 13.3% on equity and 7.5% on total capital.

Using Areas of Current Strength as a Criterion

A third popular approach to setting investment priorities is to select areas of current strength. In quantitative terms, this means market share; in more qualitative terms, it may mean that you have a unique patent, product, or marketing skill.

Although good position and unique strengths do have a high correlation with success, you must once again take into account that what contributed to successes in the past may not do so in the future and that the market you serve may actually be in a state of rapid decline.

Using Combinations of These Approaches

The limitations of each of these approaches have caused some people to use more than one approach: Some combine growth with position (see Figure 3–1), others combine return on investment with growth, and still others use all three. This in turn has led to the use of matrixes that depict these situations. Let's look at how you can put these to work. No one would disagree that segments of a business with high growth (10% and up), strong position (25% and up), and high ROI (15% and up) have high investment potential and that they deserve a high portion of the available investment dollars, or that those segments that score poorly in all these categories should be carefully scrutinized and given a low credit rating. Nevertheless, a word of caution is required: To be truly useful, these figures must be projected forward, and they will only be as good as the data and assumptions that underlie them. If they are merely extrapolations of the past, they can be very misleading.

Furthermore, you must understand other dimensions of the market—competition, technology, and sociopolitical conditions that can influence growth, position, and profitability. As a result, more qualitative evaluation systems have been

Figure 3-1. Plotting industries in relation to your historical profit and sales growth.

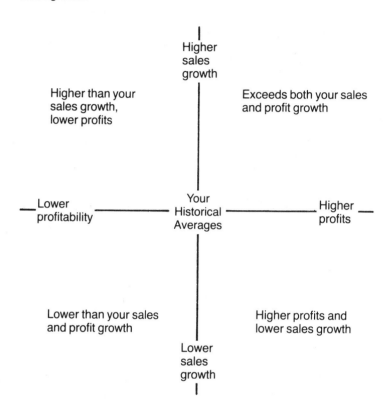

developed to determine the present and future attractiveness of the industry and your relative strengths and limitations. Like all other systems, this one has its assets and liabilities, and it must be handled and implemented with sound judgment.

How to Determine Attractiveness

The Nature of the Market

One important factor in determining attractiveness is the market's size, cyclicality, and sensitivity—not just its growth. A market that grows very rapidly for a year, then takes a dive only to grow again during the third year may *not* be attractive, even if *on the average* its growth is above 10%. A market which is very small isn't as attractive as a large market, since the returns may not justify the investment required. A highly price-sensitive, energy-sensitive, or "government-sensitive" market may also be less attractive. Therefore, the first question for managers to ask is what is attractive to them—which areas are critical and outweigh the rest? I have known some companies that wouldn't invest in any market worth less than $500 million. Some seek out a portfolio of countercyclical or complementary cyclicalities—that is, markets that decline at a different time than other markets in which the business participates. For example, if a company has a large number of consumer businesses, it might wish to invest in industrial markets that decline and expand before or after the consumer markets. Other companies will only consider low price-sensitive markets. Thus, what is attractive to one management team is unacceptable to another.

The Competitive Environment

A second dimension in determining relative attractiveness is the competitive climate. Some companies thrive in a highly concentrated industry, whereas others require fragmentation. Concentration or lack of concentration may affect industry stability and pricing practices. Without a market leader, there may be constant chaos. This can be measured merely by determining what percentage of the market is controlled by the top three firms or by seeing how many companies must be included to reach 70% of the market. There are some companies that win against small single-industry competitors and lose against multi-industry giants, whereas others do the opposite. A rapid change in competitors, in which many leave and others enter the market all at once, can mean a totally unmanageable situation for some and success for others.

Another aspect is worth considering here: If you have become accustomed to a stable and gentlemanly competitive situation and if you are contemplating entering one in which the competition is more aggressive—even cutthroat—then be prepared for a "culture shock," and proceed with caution. Thus, you can see that competitive preference is variable and can make the difference between success and failure. And it involves more than just market share; you must identify your own preferences as well.

Technological Change

A third factor that should be considered is technological change. Some industries have mature, slowly changing technologies, and this is considered to be highly attractive; others are on the opposite end of the spectrum, and they have their advocates as well. Ultimately technology can be translated into protectability and capital need and risk. A new patent-protectable technology can be a significant asset and can even provide a "competitive advantage" for the innovator—if he knows what to do with it. This can make the industry unattractive to those who feel that they *must* be the market leader, but it can be very profitable for those who are willing to accept second or third place and who can selectively target those segments that are left unattended or are considered too small for the giant.

Another factor in this innovative situation is whether the product is truly protectable for a significant period. If it can be copied or if the patents can be easily bypassed, then it may not be attractive to the leader or to the followers. Another consideration is if there is the possibility of cross-licensing or licensing from the leader. In that case, other factors—such as marketing, manufacturing, or financing skills—may be more decisive than the innovation itself.

A mature technological state may be either highly attractive or unattractive, depending on your perceptions or desires. Maturity permits standardization and thus yields opportunities for cost reduction. It may cause the winner to be more effective in other aspects of the business; but it may also be undesirable because the product becomes a commodity—that is, it cannot be differentiated by the customer because all the products are perceived to be similar. Sugar, coffee, and gasoline are commodities, but in each case manufacturers have worked hard to make the consumer believe there are product differences. If this can't be done, there will be profit pressure because of aggressive price competition.

Before I discuss other factors that affect the investment attractiveness of a business or segment, I would like to point out that innovation also pertains to process and manufacturing technology. In some mature products, there is a need for investing in automation or in expensive information systems, and this may determine the relative attractiveness of making that investment. For example, in some areas of consumer distribution there is a need for up-to-date communications and data processing equipment. This is expensive, and has dramatically increased the cost of being a distributor. The expense includes software development as well as equipment rentals, and software is often the most expensive element and requires the most expertise.

Financial Consideration

Investment decisions must consider the potential financial returns. Business still comes down to profitability and cash flow, although all businessmen don't have the same criteria for what constitutes success. (If they did, then no one would invest in low-margin businesses, for example.) Financial decisions must consider the nature of the front-end investment and continuing financing. If a business has low entry costs, or if the required investment is low because of third party financing or tax advantages, then it may be highly attractive despite lower returns on investment. In some businesses all the investment is made by the government, and the ROI is extremely attractive. Industries also vary in the amount of cash flow. Some have excellent cash turnovers, whereas others require considerable investment in receivables and inventories. The timing of returns also varies: In some businesses, it takes years; in others, returns occur rapidly. Obviously there are significant differences in risk: Some investments are like receiving annuities, whereas others are like betting on the long shot in a horse race. In short, some industries have high ROI and low ROS (return on sales), whereas others are the opposite.

The Manufacturing Process

The attractiveness of an investment is related to the nature and complexity of the manufacturing required. Some industries thrive on complexity, unique processes, and long-cycle manufacturing and require a great deal of front-end capital and experience; others require simplicity, short cycles, and ease of entry. There are even those that require the ability to do little or no manufacturing on their own, marketing a source product manufactured by another company. Some industries permit small, flexible, on-site manufacturing; others, due to economy-of-scale production or the cost of facilities, require extreme centralization.

Some industries require extensive backward integration—as far back as the source of raw material. This means that if you wish to participate successfully, you must operate mines, transportation systems, refineries, and so on. Finally, there is the factor of unionization. In some industries you must deal with strong, militant unions on a national level. Many managers see unionization as unattractive, although a few seem to believe that unions serve a useful function in keeping the workforce in line and providing labor stability.

Sociopolitical and Economic Factors

In the previous chapter I suggested that you determine the impact of macroenvironmental forces on your markets, industry, and competition. These factors can influence the attractiveness of a market, industry, and business, and they can change rapidly along with changing conditions. For example, in the Cold War era, industries related to national defense were supportive of social and governmental actions, but ten years later they were opposed to many of those actions, and today they are largely neutral. You must ask yourself if you prefer to have your industry strongly, moderately, or negatively responsive to these macroenvironmental factors.

How to Use the Attractiveness Screen

Categorize the Market

The first step is to segment the business by deciding how you wish to categorize the market and the product. This categorization is a result of the costs of doing business or producing the product. Markets can be divided in the following manner:

Location: Worldwide, regions, urban centers, populations—for example:
Developed nations, developing nations, underdeveloped nations
Europe, Africa, Americas, Asia
Northeast, East, South . . .
Cities with populations over 1,000,000; those with populations of 500,000–1,000,000 . . .
Eastern Corridor . . .

Purchasing Behavior: Size and frequency of purchase, degree of centralization in decision making, channels of purchase, desire to lease vs. desire to buy—for example:
Customers who buy once a year, twice a year . . .
Orders of over $1,000,000 . . .
National, regional, local purchasing decisions
Direct purchase, wholesale distributor
Purchases, retail purchases
Full-lease, lease/buy-back, direct purchase

Product Use: End user, applications, degree of experience, service requirements, quality/reliability needs—for example:
Users in metal, petroleum, mining industries
Applications for finance, inventory . . .
Novices, intermediates, professionals . . .
Partial service required, full service, "do-it-yourselfers"
Those requiring 100% reliability, 75% minimum . . .

Customer Characteristics: Size, diversity of investment, strategy integration, financial condition—for example:
  Large multi-product producers, small specialists
  Customers growing, holding, harvesting
  Fully integrated, partially integrated
  Triple A credit rating, Double A . . .

The key is to select the categorization that can give you insight into the size, growth, and competitive position of the particular business in which you would like to invest. Products can be divided up as follows:

Material Used (e.g., metal, wood, plastics)
Size or Power (e.g., tonnage, horsepower)
Model (e.g., deluxe, standard)
Manufacturing Process (e.g., handcrafted, standard, automated)

These should help you determine the cost and complexity of the product.
A business segment describes both of these dimensions. Figure 3–2 shows how you might segment two industries—automobiles (according to size and region) and furniture (according to manufacturing process and location of use).

Set Criteria for Attractiveness

Determine what you believe constitutes high, medium, and low attractiveness in each area: What is an attractive market, competitive situation, technology, manufacturing process, and level of profitability? Remember that this should reflect *your* preferences and that it will vary from individual to individual. It will also be helpful if you check with your superiors, associates, and subordinates to obtain their perspectives. This may modify your criteria, but even if it doesn't you will know how your perceptions vary from theirs. You will then be able to set criteria for evaluating each of your current segments and any others you may wish to evaluate.

Figure 3-2. Possible ways of segmenting the automobile and furniture industries.

AUTOMOBILES

	East	Central	South	West
Large-size				
Medium-size				
Compact				

FURNITURE

	Living Room	Dining Room	Recreation Room	Bedroom
Handcrafted (custom-made)				
Standard (made to order)				
Off the shelf (from stock)				

Use these criteria to determine how attractive the *segment* has been and is now, and how attractive it will be in the future. Then record each segment, as in Figure 3–3.

Evaluating Your Position in the Segment

Now you are ready to move into the second phase of the evaluation—determining your own relative position or

Figure 3-3. Attractiveness of automobiles of various sizes in urban, suburban, and rural markets.

	Urban	Suburban	Rural
Large	Low	Medium	High
Medium	Medium	High	Medium
Compact	High	Medium	Low

abilities compared to those of your competition. In other words, what are your relative strengths and limitations?

Marketing Position

How do you compare with your competitors in your ability to anticipate change, convince the customer to buy your product, promote your product, teach customers how to use the product, and provide service? This may require a comparison of market share, sales coverage, advertising budget and effectiveness, the extent of distribution and service, and the value of the brand. Are you strong or weak in these areas?

Technological Position

How do you compare in your ability to do basic and advanced research? How do you compare in designing and moving the product into production? Do you have the image of a leader or follower? What about your patent position, the extent and sophistication of your laboratories, your coverage of technologies, funding, and so on?

Production Position

Are you the manufacturing process leader? Do you have a strong cost position? What about your capacity, plant, location, flexibility, and labor relations as compared with those of your competitors?

Financial Position

What is your financial situation? Have you been making the same returns as your competitors, or are yours higher (lower)? What about your cash and capital position and credit/financial rating? Does your financial position provide any competitive advantage or disadvantage? Also, will any macroenvironmental trends have a greater or lesser impact on you than on your key competitors?

Overall Position

The process is the same as I recommend in the attractiveness evaluation:

1. *Evaluate each segment.*
2. *Be objective in your assessment.* Remember that it is relative and will only help you if you compare yourself accurately with your competitors. The criteria should be the same. Figure 3–4 illustrates what I mean.
3. *Understand what motivates and drives the competitor.* For a multi-industry, diversified company, this will include a summary of the parent company's key problems, financial objectives, and corporate leadership. In other words, you should reconstruct the total corporate profile so that you will be able to determine whether your competitor is a sales-, margin-, or cash-generator for the parent. This may help explain why your competitor behaves differently than you do. Furthermore, you should note how the competitor's assets reinforce the strengths of the component in the segment being evaluated.

Another point is to recognize both the positive and the

Figure 3-4. Overall attractiveness and position evaluation of automobiles of various sizes in urban, suburban, and rural markets.

	Urban	Suburban	Rural
Large-size	<u>Low</u> Medium	<u>Medium</u> Weak	<u>High</u> Strong
Medium-size	<u>Medium</u> Strong	<u>High</u> Strong	<u>Medium</u> Weak
Compact	<u>High</u> Weak	<u>Medium</u> Weak	<u>Low</u> Medium

negative impact of a foreign government on your competitor. For instance, a foreign government may provide R&D funds or financial support, but its full-employment, lifetime-work guarantees may be a detriment to the company. In short, recognize the *total* competitor, not just the single aspect you meet in the marketplace.

4. On the basis of an assessment of your assets and limitations compared to those of your competitors, you should *determine your overall strengths and limitations*—past and present.

5. Next, *project how your current strategy will contribute to an improved, stable, or declining position.* This is a critical step and one that is often overlooked. It acknowledges that your strengths and weaknesses will change, and that they are a result of your own actions.

Suppose that in recent years your company has had a superior manufacturing position. This may have been because a decade ago the company invested in a new state-of-the-art facility with sophisticated equipment, and this investment permitted higher productivity and lower costs. But let's also assume that your objective, realistic assessment is that the strategy of the past five years has been one of harvesting your

Figure 3-5. A market-growth/share matrix.

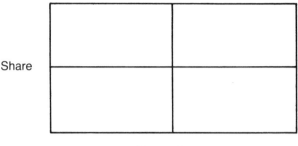

Share

Market Growth

established position. Therefore, you may conclude that if the harvesting continues and investments are accelerated, then your position will erode and you will fall from a superior to a moderate or parity position. This same kind of assessment should be completed for all functional areas.

The Use of Matrixes

All of these approaches lend themselves to the use of simple or complex matrixes to demonstrate current, future, and strategic alternatives. The use of market-growth and share matrixes, shown in Figure 3–5, is promoted by some. If plotted for each segment or product, this diagram can show the company whether its portfolio is growing, holding steady, or declining. ROI/growth or ROS/ROI matrixes, or other combinations, can also be useful.

The attractiveness/position plot can also be used to show current, future, and strategic choices. Figure 3–6 shows a business strongly positioned in an attractive industry, but whose current strategy will reduce its position while the industry itself will become less attractive.

Remember that this is the consequence of the changing environment, which may be inevitable or beyond one's control, and the impact of past strategy, which is within one's control. The question is, will management be content with the

Figure 3-6. An attractiveness/position matrix for a company whose current strategy will reduce its position while the industry is also becoming less attractive.

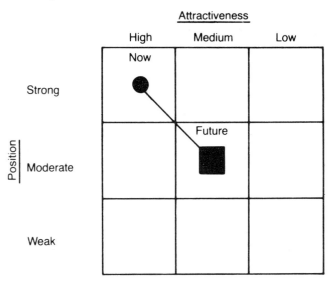

current situation, or will it want to take action that will prevent its loss of position? It may even want to do something dynamic to maintain its position and attractiveness. Each of these decisions has different consequences and will require a different investment strategy, as is illustrated in Figure 3–7.

Management Strategy Selection

Decision matrixes are useful displays and decision tools to help you determine where you are now, and where you want to be in the future, but they don't help you determine how to get there.

If you are going to grow or increase your share, will you accomplish this best by innovation, marketing, or manufacturing, or by executive- and financial-driven strategies and programs? The same question must be answered whether you intend to hold or to harvest.

Figure 3-7. Attractiveness/position matrixes showing different investment strategies. **A** illustrates a strategy of harvesting. **B** shows a company's attempt to stop erosion and hold its relative position, even though the environment is becoming less attractive. In **C**, the company is aggressively attempting to forestall its loss of attractiveness, although this may be beyond the capability of any one company. Codes:
● = current position; ■ = future position (if strategy remains same);
★ = strategic position desired.

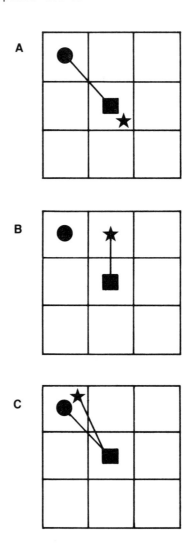

The selection of the management strategy or driver isn't a simple task. As in all phases of strategic thinking, you must analyze and evaluate your relative position. There are three ways to make the selection: First, identify and build on your strengths; second, aim at forcing the current leader to underutilize his strengths; or third, you can aim at creating a new set of success factors that change the rules of the game.

Build on Strengths

Obviously the best driver is based on the unique strengths that you already possess. Suppose that you have a unique engineering staff with an innovative track record, and that because of its talent your company was the innovator that developed the market—this very uniqueness should be the foundation of your future strategy. Or you may have developed a strong distribution and dealer network; in that case, a marketing/distribution driver may make the most sense. But it must always be kept in mind that yesterday's strength could be tomorrow's limitation. For example, your innovation may have been based on mechanical technologies, but the future may require electronic technologies. You may have a small, specialized, conservative dealer network, but the future may depend on large generalists. Thus, uniqueness must conform with the environment and be relative to present and future competition.

Play on Your Competitors' Weaknesses

Another way to select the driver is to evaluate the current market leaders and pinpoint their limitations. This insight can then help you develop a strategic thrust that aims at those identified weaknesses and forces the competitor to divert his attention from building on his strengths to correcting his limitations. For example, there are many companies whose success has been based on innovative, state-of-the-art products. These companies are often led by entrepreneurial inventors who are so enamored of the product itself that they neglect the market and business aspects. Thus, they may not have a strong, efficient manufacturing and distribution system and, as a result, may be high-cost producers. Therefore, you may decide upon a marketing or manufacturing driver that will allow you to gain cost or market position. And, by attacking the leader's weakness, you may in turn force him to allocate less for product innovation.

The opposite may also be the case—the competitor may lack the ability to innovate, and you can force him to play by your rules. It is important to remember that all companies, even the perennial winners, have limitations. Illustrations are numerous:

—For many years, Volkswagen successfully took advantage of General Motors' and Ford's preoccupation with large, stylized automobiles. Instead of trying to compete with the stylistic features of its American competitors, Volkswagen emphasized economy and performance features. But later the tables were turned when Japanese small-car manufacturers, taking advantage of Volkswagen's unwillingness to make annual style changes, displaced Volkswagen as leaders of the small-car market. General Motors tried to duplicate its success by introducing the Corvair and the Vega, but these models were so unsuccessful that after a few years they were both discontinued.

—Over two decades ago, IBM emphasized leasing, applications, and service to displace the product innovator, Remington Rand, in main-frame computers. Remington Rand was an engineering- and product-focused company that had developed the first UNIVAC computer. It lacked full appreciation of the computer's commercial value and seriously underestimated its market potential. The company apparently believed that computer users would buy on the technical merits of the computer, while IBM recognized that computers could be sold with a combination of service and financing. IBM fielded a large service organization that worked closely with the customer to develop software and extend the applications and usage across the business. Leasing reduced the risk and capital requirements for the customer. In this way the technical follower became and has remained the undisputed leader against all competition. This is an excellent example of a combined management strategy, with a close, consistent coupling of implementation programs.

Capitalize on Environmental Changes

A third approach to developing a management strategy is to carefully examine external environmental changes and build the thrust to capitalize on them. In this case, we use our evaluations of the customer, market, sociopolitical, and industry trends. As businesses and products move along the life cycle (i.e., from rapid to slow growth, to stability and decline), new thrusts become appropriate.

For example, in an early stage, the customer may have had difficulty selecting and using the product. Recognizing this need, the market leader may have built his thrust on service and applications know-how (as in the IBM approach just described); you may have followed. But now that the customer knows what he wants, the thrust may change to price or to more sophisticated product configurations. Governmental regulations may make it possible for you to become an innovator in providing products that help implement these regulations, and instead of building your strategy around distribution, you may wish to move aggressively toward becoming the service leader. Cost acceleration may dictate that you drive your business along manufacturing efficiency, rather than according to market development modes.

In summary, management strategy determines what will be the major thrust of the business in achieving its investment and profit objectives. Management strategy depends on the analyses that you already completed, and it is a result of:

A unique, unchallenged strength of your own.
A flaw or weakness you have detected in your competitor.
New market, customer, or environmental changes.

Implementation Strategy

After you have determined your investment priorities and have selected the appropriate management strategy, you must evaluate *all* the critical and supportive programs that will help implement your strategy. The key ingredients are surfacing *all* functional programs—including technical, production, marketing, and finance—and making sure that they are consistent and integrated.

Critical programs are a direct result of decisions that you made previously. What is critical for growth through innovation may be unimportant for growth via marketing. A holding strategy based on manufacturing efficiency will have different functional needs than a harvesting strategy based on price, and this will vary from one business segment to another.

I have found two approaches especially useful in developing implementation strategies. One focuses on rapid identification of the critical success factors; the second evaluates and describes *all* the functional decisions, and then identifies the most critical. Both provide insight about what functional strategies need to be changed and how likely it is that the strategy will be a success.

Approach I: Identifying Critical Factors

This approach starts with a specification of the opportunity/segment, including what the opportunity is, when and where it will take place, how big it is expected to be, and the investment and management strategies selected to pursue the opportunity.

For example, a company may decide to penetrate the high-fashion men's market and, by introducing new styles every two years, increase its share from 10% to 25% of the available market by mid-1980.

The next step is to identify the critical resources required to achieve the desired results in the time specified. One of the most important of these is *marketing skills* such as specialty-, fashion-, and service-oriented dealers to whom you will sell directly; salesmen who understand the particular segment with which they are dealing; and advertising geared to your specific clientele. Another important resource is *production skills.* For the example cited above, that would include quality tailoring, handicraft skills, and access to quality fabrics.

Creativity is yet another critical resource. In this particular case, it would mean fashion designers who can create a unique style to stimulate demand.

The third step in this approach is a careful and critical assessment of your current skills and know-how. You must ask yourself if you have the talent, equipment, facilities, and materials to carry out your goals. Finally, you must specify *how* your available skills, talents, and facilities will be used, and how those that are not available at all will be obtained, be it through acquisition, subcontracting, upgrading, joint developing, or some other means.

This approach requires considerable insight, since it rapidly focuses on those resources that will separate the "winners" from the "losers." Thus, it is most suitable for situations where the market is already in existence or where role models can be identified. One of the best ways to identify these factors is to study the current leaders and analyze what has contributed to their success. The danger, however, is that the factors required for future success may be significantly different from those required for past success.

Suppose that the available resources don't match the required resources, and that the ones that are needed can't be obtained: This could mean that your strategy and objectives, or both, are unrealistic and need to be reexamined. Thus, this could serve as a test to evaluate the viability of your strategy.

Approach II: Evaluation of All Functional Programs

The second approach is more comprehensive and detailed. Like the first approach, it begins with a specification of the segment and an evaluation of both investment and management strategy. Then it goes on to list *all* the functional decisions and programs that are required for implementation. In marketing, for example, you would describe the product-planning and management, distribution, promotion, pricing, service, sales, and intelligence-gathering strategies. For manufacturing you would describe the facility plans and the extent of automation, quality control, materials, procurement, and so on. Engineering and technical programs will then be outlined to include the specific research, development, and production engineering required to implement the strategy.

In each case you should describe the kind of programs you think are necessary to successfully implement the strategies you have chosen. For example, a harvesting strategy distribution contraction requires a different program than does a holding strategy based on the production of quality products. (This will be discussed further in Chapter 8.)

Once you have decided upon your ideal program, you should then compare the realities with your ideal to determine their compatibility. You may be using specialty distribution when general distribution is preferred. You may be pricing on cost when you should be pricing on contribution margin.* Your engineering department may be trying to develop new features when it should be aiming at increased standardization. When you have completed this assignment, you will have a listing of *all* your programs and a clearer understanding of what needs to be changed. These programs can then be listed in order of importance. Thus, you will still be aiming at the most critical factors, but you will have a description of *all* the supportive programs as well. (See Chapter 9.)

Once you know what needs to be continued and changed, you can probe further to determine if you possess all the critical resources necessary to do the job. If some are missing, then you should determine how they can be obtained. The results are the same as in Approach I, but Approach II is more comprehensive. It is best suited for situations in which you are thinking about making a significant change in strategy or are considering entering a new market or segment.

Who Is Responsible for What?

Investment-level decisions are the sole responsibility of those individuals who know what the corporate resource base is and will be—the chief executive officer or those designated

---

* Contribution margin is gross sales minus direct labor, materials, and directly related overhead expenses.

as the Executive Office or Policy Committee. Their responsibility includes determining the criteria to be used in making these decisions: Only they can decide what is a truly attractive situation and how strong they should be to capitalize on it. But they need help—in determining what is happening and what is likely to happen in all environmental areas; in evaluating themselves in relation to their competition; and in surfacing changes in either environment, competition, or resources, which may cause investments to move from one area to another or may make yesterday's success tomorrow's failure. This help can be obtained from other senior executives, high-level staff, or outside consultants. The more a business needs to change, the more it requires an outside view. If the management is too close to the situation because of its own past experiences, it should enlist the help of others.

After the CEO has decided where to invest and how much, the decision-making responsibility will move down the organizational ladder. Management strategy decision making is the domain of the business manager. He or she is closest to the microenvironment and is in the best position to determine the most appropriate driver. This decision, however, should be reviewed at the next level of management to test its viability. The business manager requires the input of lower-level managers, especially those who may be able to identify a competitive weakness or environmental change that can provide the basis of a successful thrust. For example, an engineering manager may spot a competitor's product that has poor reliability or a high failure rate, while a marketing manager may discover a flaw in the competitor's distribution or sales coverage. These individuals should be consulted in developing and selecting the management strategy.

Implementation strategy must be developed by the functional experts with input from specialists, but these individuals may have difficulty determining the critical factors that can make the difference—this will require review and assessment by outsiders. This is particularly true if the segment is new or unknown to those involved. In this case, an in-depth study is required.

In short, all levels of management must play a role in the

Figure 3-8. The roles of different levels of management in the
formulation of strategy.

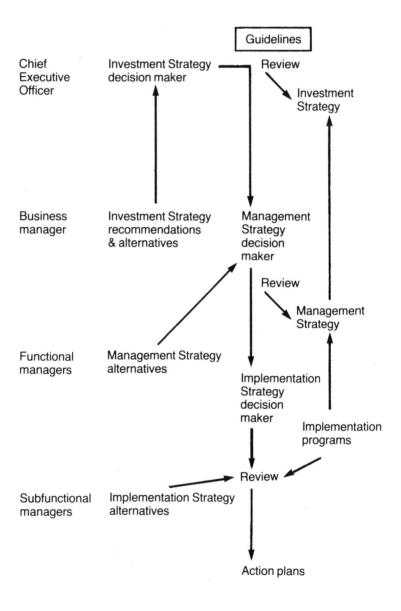

formation of strategy, either by providing inputs to a higher level of management or by reviewing strategic decisions submitted to them. Finally, they are the implementers and controllers of the decisions they have made. Figure 3–8 summarizes this series of relationships.

Strategy Review

As Figure 3–8 illustrates, the final step in strategic planning is to review the total picture and to decide if it is believable and consistent. Can the strategy achieve its promised results, or is it merely a dream? This may be determined by an examination of past results and a comparison of them with projected results. If significant improvement in sales, earnings, or cash is anticipated, then it will be useful to identify why and how this will occur. Is a major innovation that was promised for years finally expected to take place? If so, why will it happen in the forecasted period? If the share has slowly eroded but is now expected to increase, what makes this assessment believable?

This is commonly referred to as a "gap analysis," since it identifies and attempts to explain why the gap between present and future results will be bridged. The "how" may be based on both external and internal factors—such as market growth and competitive change—as well as on key programs such as engineering, marketing, and manufacturing. These reviews should be performed by the higher level of management or by impartial consultants, since it can't be done objectively and effectively by those who prepared the strategy in the first place. A rule of thumb is that the preparer and reviewer of the strategy should not be the same individual.

Depending on the nature of the business, the degree of change, and the complexity of the programs, special reviews may be beneficial. For instance, if the entire strategy hinges on a technological breakthrough, then it should be examined by technical experts in that specific field. If the key to success lies in penetrating a new market or an entirely different business, a review by market or industry experts may be helpful.

If the business is threatened by new legislation or legal action, then it needs the advice of legal and political specialists. The basic issue here is to determine whether resources will be available in sufficient quantity and at the right time to meet your schedule. If they won't be, then the reviewers should recommend other options or more realistic timing and implementation programs.

PART II

Successful Management
Strategies

4

Marketing-Based
Strategies

IN the last two chapters I outlined various analyses and
decision-making processes used to determine the most appropriate investment, management, and implementation
strategy. I intentionally highlighted the key steps and did not
explore all the complexities of this kind of planning. As a
result, you could have the mistaken impression that it is easy.
It isn't easy! It requires considerable thought and hard work.

In this chapter I would like to elaborate on all the
marketing-based strategies available to managers. This will be
followed in subsequent chapters with in-depth examina-
tions of manufacturing-, financial-, and innovation-based
strategies. In each case I will attempt to outline how these
strategies will vary depending on whether the investment
strategy is aimed at growth, holding, declining, or exiting.
Then I will describe specific situations in which the strategy

may be appropriate to consider along with the critical success factors, the implications of implementation strategies, and other key programs.

I hope to provide you with a way of describing your current strategy and to offer you a means of developing sound and practical alternatives. I am focusing on the management strategy or key driver since it is a critical step that is often overlooked in the strategic planning process. Often managers skip from the investment to the implementation area without consciously deciding upon the thrust of the business. This step also provides the largest number of options.

In the first chapter I outlined five marketing-based strategies:

Need/want identification
Demand-influencing
Distribution/dealer-focused
Service/application-directed
Geographic/segment extension or contraction

I shall now discuss each of these in some detail.

Need/Want Identification Strategies

This strategy aims at surfacing and meeting latent needs and wants either by developing an entirely new product or by adapting an existing product to meet changed needs. Often the customer or user of the product may not recognize that there is a need and may not be able to articulate it. Thus, you must be able not only to meet the need but also to convince the customer that he or she needs the product.

SITUATION I: LEADER RECOGNIZES NEED
FOR IMPROVING PRODUCT

In this case the industry or segment leader is content with his position and desires to protect it. Furthermore, he recognizes that the product can become obsolete if he doesn't continue to improve it and make it more useful to customers. Thus, he systematically evaluates how well the product is functioning and identifies specific areas in which improvement can be made.

Du Pont, for instance, was the product innovator in developing non-stick surfaces. It introduced Teflon in 1961 and remained the quality leader, although there were many imitations. As is often the case, the imitators competed on the basis of price. But Du Pont soon noticed a deficiency in its product—Teflon wore off after three years. Fifteen years later, in 1976, Du Pont introduced a longer-lasting, higher-quality non-stick coating—Silvertone. As is typical of Du Pont, it has restricted the use of this new coating to high-quality cookware, thereby reinforcing the company's quality image. Later on, it will probably introduce this coating to its medium-price merchandise and will ultimately license it to other manufacturers who serve the low- as well as medium- and high-price segments. Thus, Du Pont is able to maintain its quality and innovation status and at the same time force its price-oriented competitors to play catch-up ball.

SITUATION II: NEW ENTRY SURFACES A NEED IGNORED BY MARKET LEADER

Marcel Bich, founder and chief executive officer of Société Bic, has had a simple and yet remarkably successful strategy aimed at filling the consumer's desire for relatively inexpensive *disposable* products. *Business Week* pointed out several interesting aspects of his strategy: "Bich's products are not his inventions. Rather than innovate, he relies on improving products and marketing them worldwide. For example, he developed a world market for a disposable razor, a product that has been around for years." * His strategy has been successfully applied to pens, lighters, and panty hose, as well as razors. In each case Bic has taken on the larger, more entrenched competitor.

* *Business Week,* February 28, 1977.

In the case of disposable razors Bic had to compete directly with the market leader, Gillette. Gillette has a highly successful track record and had won against Schick and even Philip Morris, the owner of Personna brand. Gillette was, however, not particularly interested in developing a market for a cheap, fully disposable razor, since this would reduce the sales of its traditional and highly profitable replacement-blade business. So Bic focused on the leader's weakness and reluctance to carve out this niche for itself. In the disposable lighter market Bic and Gillette also competed head on, and again Bic was able to take a slight lead in early 1978.

This illustrates how a strategy can be used to penetrate a market which had been dominated by one company and in which all previous attempts had been unsuccessful. Of course, it also exemplifies a situation in which the leader has a real problem: If Gillette is successful in introducing a disposable razor, then it will only move sales from one of its products to another; if it fails, it will lose total position. Thus, a new product with different features can be a powerful way of gaining market position. Bich's strategy also points out how the total strategy must be taken into consideration. Bich supports his marketing thrust with heavy advertising and increased capacity in advance of the anticipated demand. Without these supporting elements Bich would have been less successful.

In 1975 a tremendous growth of sales of electronic digital watches caused considerable anxiety for traditional watch manufacturers. Digital displays became very popular and caught consumer's imagination. But a year later the electronic watch manufacturers were confronted with a problem: The batteries of their watches weren't strong enough to last even for the year that was promised. This led to a race among electronic watch manufacturers to come up with a better, longer-lasting battery. *Business Week* reported that National Semiconductor was introducing a lithium battery-powered watch "aimed at leapfrogging its competition and getting back into the mainstream digital watch business. . . . It has already signed exclusive manufacturing deals with two companies, Eagle-Picher Industries, Inc., and Honeywell, Inc.

that now produce lithium batteries for space and military applications." * This is an excellent example of how an improved product can be used to move ahead of the competition and of how it can be done by using a technology developed for another purpose.

The need for labor-saving processes is common in industrial companies. One area is the labor cost of assembling the cartons used to ship products. Stolman Corporation developed a machine which makes boxes that can be more easily assembled, thus reducing labor costs for the companies that use the box. This is an illustration of how this strategic approach can help meet the needs of an industrial customer.

Hundreds of illustrations could be cited, ranging from the annual feature additions on cars and motorcycles to the more automated versions of traditional machine tools. In each successful case the situation was based on a customer's need or desire that was significant enough to help a company gain or hold its market position. This strategy requires sound market research and product planning, along with a willingness to invest heavily in front-end development and possibly to suffer losses. It also recognizes that success may take time and that customers must be given time to learn how to use the product at a minimum risk. In the consumer area this may take the form of low prices or money-back guarantees; in an industrial situation it could mean considerable training, comprehensive demonstrations, and possibly trial periods or lease agreements.

In terms of organization, this strategy must closely integrate marketing, product planning, and engineering, especially in the early stages. Many companies have installed matrix management organization to increase integration. Under this organizational approach, a project or product manager is appointed to plan, organize, control, and measure the new product. He or she normally reports to the general manager or, in a smaller company, directly to the chief executive officer. The project manager has a small staff and uses the professional resources of each function. The functional man-

* *Business Week*, February 28, 1977.

ager (engineering, manufacturing, or sales) is responsible for
the professional performance of his people, and they report
to him on a solid-line basis and a dotted-line basis to the
project manager. By solid line I mean that the professional
engineer, salesman, and manufacturing specialist is paid and
rewarded by the functional manager to whom he reports but
gets direction from the project manager. The project manager appraises and guides the specialist and has an input into
his or her performance appraisal, thus influencing salary increases and promotions. Normally, the professional engineer
and others are assigned to a number of projects but have only
one functional manager.

This illustrates how organization is adapted to fit strategy
and meet changing business needs. The professionals only
work on the project as needed, and this reduces the problem
of having to lay off professionals when their services aren't
required. However, this organizational concept isn't a
panacea, and it must be monitored periodically.

Demand-Influencing Strategies

The marketing-driven strategy I just described is aimed at
satisfying a need that already exists and that is recognized by
the customer. There have been many situations in which this
need wasn't perceived and in which the customer had no
recognition of it at first. This doesn't mean that the customer
was manipulated, but rather that the strategist spent considerable time creating, accelerating, or enhancing that recognition. Demand can be created in a variety of ways, but from a
marketing point of view promotion and pricing seem to be
the most successful means.

How Promotion Influences Demand

SITUATION I: DEVELOPING A MARKET FOR A NEW PRODUCT
OR SERVICE

Mr. Coffee, an unknown, one-product company, singlehandedly built a market for a specific kind of coffee maker,
that had been used in Europe but was not that popular in the

United States. Its strategy was based on saturation advertising in all media. For its spokesman the company used Joe DiMaggio, who has an image and reputation for honesty and credibility. From nowhere, Mr. Coffee created a demand and became number one. In fact, its name became synonymous with the product and although all large manufacturers followed its lead, the Mr. Coffee brand is still the best known.

Situation II: Adding New Life to Existing Products

New interest in existing products can be nurtured, as exemplified by packaged food companies and consumer paper product leaders such as General Mills, General Foods, and Procter and Gamble. These companies have been able to continue and accelerate interest in consumer goods by extensive advertising, product promotion, in-store displays, special introductory offers, and attractive packaging.

This approach is also common in the cigarette industry, where brand awareness has been a critical element, and Philip Morris has attempted to use this approach in the beer industry by spending an estimated $3 per barrel on advertising and sales promotion, three times the industry average. With this level of expenditure it has been able to move Miller to a strong number three position, increasing its share at the expense of Anheuser-Busch and Schlitz. This aggressive penetration strategy via promotion has caused Miller to lose money during the five years that it has been owned by Philip Morris. This points out the need to be willing to suffer short-term losses for the sake of long-term profitability.

Situation III: The Need to Protect Your Image

Advertising- and promotion-driven strategies may be required to protect your image and reputation. Many forces require a company to maintain its "customer franchise." We all know that customers have a short memory and that unless we continue to remind them of our products they will forget and switch their loyalties. In addition, there are groups that try to separate the consumer or user from the manufacturer—for instance, in consumer products there are wholesalers and retailers. Many of these are large and wish to develop their own "franchises" with the customer. In some cases they use their own brands, instead of the manufacturer's brand. (Sears is the most successful retailer in the use of its own brand.) Because of the proliferation of these groups, manufacturers are often forced into an aggressive brand- and image-building strategy. Some companies have resisted the private-label trend and have been unwilling to sell products to those who demand their own labels.

But national promotion strategies are being increasingly adopted by industrial-focused companies as well. Several unknown brands have aggressively promoted their names in the office copier business. Savin Business Machines has used this approach in its attempt to gain share at the expense of Xerox, and Addressograph-Multigraph has followed its lead.

Hence, demand-creating promotion can be used to gain or hold share in both consumer and industrial markets. But there are several conditions that must be met:

1. The product must meet the expectations that the promotion creates. If the promotion emphasizes product quality and durability, then the product must have these characteristics. If demand is built on styling and fashion or cost savings, then these features must be built into the product.

2. The advertising media selected must be consistent with your targeted customers. If you are trying to appeal to the young, sports-minded, affluent male, or to the chic female consumer, then the medium you choose should be one that appeals to these groups, not one that appeals to other segments of the population. This criterion of appropriateness should help you decide whether to use print or visual media, on a national or regional basis. At times these choices aren't obvious, and outside consulting help may be required.

3. You must be prepared to meet the demand in a timely manner. This requires appropriate levels of inventory and warehousing and prompt delivery. There is no greater waste of money than to create demand and then lack sufficient inventory to meet the customer's needs. This will permit the

competition to move in and sell his product, even though he might have invested less in creating demand.

4. Consistent and adequate financing of the promotional effort is required. A blitzkrieg will certainly build interest for a period of time, but unless it is periodically reinforced, the customer will forget, and once again competition will be the big winner.

5. Management must understand the rewards, costs, and risks of this strategic thrust. Results may be slow to materialize and at times the approach will fail. But under these circumstances, management must be patient and have realistic expectations.

How Pricing Influences Demand

In addition to advertising and promotion, pricing has been used by many businesses to create, stabilize, or limit demand. These strategies can be based on the use of high, medium, or low pricing.

HIGH-PRICING STRATEGIES

Situation I. In discussing need identification I pointed out how Du Pont tends to price on the high side and preserve its product innovations on the high end. This is an excellent way to *preserve its quality image,* since most individuals equate high price with premium products. All companies that concentrate on this segment of their markets follow this approach, including Mercedes, Cadillac, Maytag, and Sony. This approach allows them to provide high margins to their dealers and helps create a snob appeal for their products.

Situation II. Another reason to become a high-priced company is if you have more demand than your *limited supply* can satisfy, and if you have no desire to add more supply. Obviously you can't overprice the product but you can hold out for more than is customary. This has been the approach used in times of scarcity by most short-cycle, supply-constrained industries. The most obvious example is that of the OPEC cartel during the oil shortage.

Situation III. If you have monopolistic control over a

product, either because you are the sole supplier or because you have a unique pattern position, then being high-priced will also work—provided that you don't create an umbrella that encourages substitute products to enter and gain a foothold in your market.

MODERATE-PRICING STRATEGIES

Moderate-pricing strategies are normally reserved for those who wish to hold or defend their position. They closely monitor their competitors and know exactly at what point they should follow or temporarily take a leadership role. Normally the thrust is to have the competitive situation determined by other factors—such as product distribution and promotion—not on the basis of price.

LOW- OR AGGRESSIVE-PRICING STRATEGIES

Situation I. Many industries have such a high breakeven point that they must maintain a certain critical level of production or be subject to losses. This *need to increase volume* or to keep the mill operating at 80–90% of capacity causes the use of aggressive pricing that will often have detrimental effects in the long run. This is typical of the forest products industry where pricing is often used to buy volume merely to keep the mill operating. In the 1974–76 period the industry seemed to have overcome this tendency—led by International Paper's effort to improve margins—but once capacity became available again, it reverted to its previous pattern. In some seasonal businesses, price is used to "load level" the facility. This means that during periods when demand is normally weak, these companies have special sales to keep the factory loaded. This practice makes sense if the cost of closing the plant and losing skilled labor exceeds the loss the company would suffer by taking business at a discount. This is why there are often special sales on boats in the winter when the season is not conducive to buying boats. Of course, this isn't the only way to "load level" the factory; you can also build up your stock.

Situation II. Pricing is a popular way to *buy share* or to disturb the marketplace, especially if the leader has created an excessive umbrella or needs the profit from this business to support others. More than 25 years ago a new approach to retailing was created with the introduction of discounters. Companies like Masters and Korvettes in New York discovered that a large number of consumers were willing to sacrifice service and attractive stores for lower prices. They also found that their profits were higher when they increased volume greater than when merely holding prices high and selling less. This approach caused significant changes in retailing. It resulted in a loss of share for the traditional department store and in the almost complete extinction of the small retailer who emphasized margin rather than volume.

Let's look at the economics of this approach. The traditional department store and small retailer would emphasize selling. For example:

10 units at $3 (30% margin) = $30 gross profit

At the same time, the high-volume merchant may be willing to accept a 20% margin if it could sell 15 units:

15 units at $2 = $30 gross profit

Thus, both earned the same profit but one sold 50% more units at $1/3$ less the price. Furthermore, if the discounter can maintain a lower overhead and selling expense, his profits may exceed those of the traditional vendor, even though he may obtain less per unit.

But this strategy isn't reserved to the consumer goods sector alone; airlines have also begun to think this way! Some carriers have decided to go for volume and reduce their prices. An article in *Forbes* * described how Southwest Airlines had developed a very profitable regional business by concentrating on lower prices ($10–$20 below economy fare) and by providing full service but only serving cities 200–500 miles from Chicago's Midway Field.

In the computer arena, Business Systems Technology, a supplier of computer peripheral equipment, has taken on IBM by providing small and medium-size companies with

* December 1, 1975.

"plug-in" compatible products at prices 25–30% below those of IBM, while including rapid response and good service to customers. It appears that IBM is fighting back and on occasion it has met BST and other small specialists with equivalent and lower prices. This illustrates that although price can be effective in eroding the position of a giant, it can't be the only factor, since the giant can counterattack and win if it so desires, because it has tremendous resources at its disposal.

Situation III. One of the most dramatic pricing strategies is the one based on learning curve theory. This theory assumes that as volume doubles in any industry, costs decline at some predetermined rate because of learning. The amount of decrease varies from situation to situation. In some cases, for every doubling of volume, there may be a 10% decline in cost; in others, a 20% decline; and in still others, a 30% decline. Thus, if a company assumes that a new product will replicate the history of another product, it will reduce prices in anticipation of this decline, hoping to increase share and volume rapidly. In some industries, like semiconductors and integrated circuits, there is a significant *learning curve impact,* and some competitors, most notably Texas Instruments, seem to have priced accordingly. This has caused prices to tumble, not only in the component area, but also in the end products related to them. For instance, digital watches and calculators both had price declines of from 50 to 75% in less than a year. This had catastrophic results: Some companies, like Bowman, went bankrupt, and Rockwell suffered significant losses. Thus, learning curve pricing can cause significant havoc and red ink for everyone in the short range but significantly higher profits in the long range for the survivors, like Texas Instruments.

Resources Necessary to Carry Out Pricing Strategies

It is evident that pricing can help increase demand and determine share, but, as with everything else, you must have certain abilities or resources to make it work. I shall outline what is necessary for each of the three major alternatives to succeed.

HIGH-PRICING STRATEGIES

To obtain a high price you must have both a high-quality, perceived-value product and a tight control over service-prone distributors and dealers. As I said before, price is correlated with quality and status of ownership. If this isn't consistent, then current owners won't spread the word to new "status" buyers, and ultimately the price will fall. Every industry has witnessed this phenomenon: At one time Fisher was equivalent with high-fidelity quality, but Fisher lost its quality position and moved to the mid-price range. Sheraton was at one time a prestige hotel chain, but it has lost this stature and is now a mid- to low-price chain. An Oldsmobile used to be a high-status automobile; now many consider it in the same category as a Chevrolet.

Control over dealers is also essential to avoid price competition. If dealers or distributors discount heavily, then a product can lose its snob appeal and status image. For this reason many manufacturers fought to keep Fair Trade or price maintenance, because this enabled them to disenfranchise—even sue—any dealer or distributor who discounted the price below its "suggested retail price." Thus, any consumer who wanted the product acquired it on the basis of the product itself, not the price. In addition, Fair Trade protected the small dealer against the large chains.

The Fair Trade law was attacked by the mass merchants and volume retailers and was ultimately declared a restraint of trade and therefore illegal. Even so, some manufacturers have been able to select dealers who have continued this policy on an unofficial basis.

Another requirement for the success of a high-pricing strategy is the attitude of both the manufacturer and his representatives toward warranties and consumer satisfaction. The manufacturer must be willing to stand behind the product and must attempt to be the leader in guarantees. Manufacturing must consistently stress quality and resist the temptation of cost reduction and improved efficiency which may inadvertently reduce quality.

MODERATE-PRICING STRATEGIES

Moderate-pricing strategies require a strong tracking and a careful response system. The company adopting this approach must know what is going on and avoid overreacting. It should try to be consistent with the average and, if someone reduces prices, it must avoid getting into a price war.

LOW-PRICING STRATEGIES

Low-pricing strategies require a real least-cost position and a willingness to suffer temporary losses. The management must be willing to do whatever is necessary to keep costs down, and it must have a system that anticipates *total* costs and changes. The engineering and manufacturing departments must constantly look for material substitution and new labor-saving, cost-reducing methods and processes. The marketing department must seek low-cost distribution and select volume/price-sensitive dealers. If price is the driver, then *everyone* should resist overadvertising, model proliferation, and any unnecessary additions to overhead. If a competitor aggressively reduces prices, then you should rapidly reduce your prices below his, and make him suffer. This all requires a willingness to undertake risk.

Distribution/Dealer-Focused Strategies

Many successful companies have gained and held share by creating the best, most effective distribution system. Thus, the barrier was distribution versus image, price, or product. The basis premise is that the business is really local or regional rather than national, and that the user relies on a loyal, competent, effective intermediary. This strategy has several variations in the degree of control and ownership of these intermediaries. This, in turn, is quite often related to the reputation and financial strength of the product- or service-provider.

SITUATION I: UNIQUE PRODUCT, WEAK FINANCES,
AND RELATIVELY UNKNOWN BRAND

Many companies have a good, differentiable product but lack the financial resources to build their own outlets or to invest in national/regional demand creation. So they carefully line up distributors or dealers to carry their products or provide their services. If the product requires application or pre-sale instruction, or is difficult to install or repair, then it is important to seek out servicing dealers. If the product is bulky or requires large handling equipment, then distributors or dealers who have these resources are necessary. If it requires investment in inventory and you are cash-poor, then distributors who have a positive cash position are vital to you.

In this situation the distributors are normally in a position of strength and you are at a disadvantage. This is a limitation and must be recognized, but it need not be a long-term limitation. As you become recognized and financially stronger, you may counter-balance the situation and even replace the independent dealers with distributors of your own.

The type of exclusivity and the nature of the franchising agreement will also vary. Many companies have sought out individuals or local companies to represent them in a region, and they have provided these franchised agents, dealers, or distributors with some degree of exclusivity over a region. At times, this has meant exclusive use of a motif, such as Howard Johnson's; at other times this has included site location, supplies, inventory control, management and employee training, and even a total communications and management system. This is exemplified by McDonald's, which even runs its own "Hamburger University" and requires that all its franchise owners *run* the business, not only invest in it. But the ability to control franchises has come under legal attack. In 1967 the Supreme Court ruled against Schwinn & Company stating that manufacturers couldn't limit their dealers or distributors to a particular territory. In 1977, however, the court reversed its ruling and appeared to permit more control by the manufacturer. On the other hand, some companies seek out other companies and individuals that can support entire regions, thereby encouraging investors rather than working entrepreneurs.

But control varies: At times franchisers are merely members of a voluntary association. The manufacturer gives them access to the product, supports them with coop-advertising (advertising whose cost is shared with the dealer or distributor), gives them specials, and lets the dealer decide how to run the business. This arrangement often makes the franchiser more of a servant than a master. Control and cost make the franchise more valuable and assure more consistency in quality and image—thus permitting a national brand. The Holiday Inn franchise is consistent (or so the advertisement says); but it is less so than McDonald's.

But consistency will only occur if the franchising company provides a product that can be consistent—if the franchise is intimately familiar with that product; if appropriate backup and support is provided; and if the franchiser monitors the franchises and is willing to disenfranchise and even take over a poorly operating dealership.

Franchising has become popular in a variety of areas. It is estimated that there was over $200 billion in franchised sales in 1976. Many companies have sought to acquire franchises. Both Beneficial and Household Finance acquired automotive parts franchise companies. Pepsico was trying to acquire Pizza Hut. In 1977 Norton Simon added Avis to its business portfolio, which includes Canada Dry (soft drinks), Max Factor (cosmetics), Halston (fashions), Hunt-Wesson (foods), McCall's Pattern's (patterns), and Somerset Importers (spirits and wines). Food chains have been popular franchise opportunities, but over the past few years franchising has become a way of life.

SITUATION II: UNIQUE BRAND, FINANCIAL STRENGTH, AND DIFFICULTY IN MAINTAINING CONTROL

Relying on the independent dealer or distributor has its limitations, and such dependence should be avoided if at all possible. For this reason many companies have gone to great lengths to control their intermediaries by equity and even by complete ownership. It is very common to find a company that acquires its franchises and runs them itself. This increases control and avoids legal entanglements, but it isn't a utopian ideal. The professional manager may not have the status required to get the necessary community, business, or political commitments, and he may not be responsive to local conditions and changes. Another problem is that the company may lose sight of the purpose of its distribution—namely, to sell its product—and become so enamored of the distribution profits that it may price itself out of the market or antagonize the customer. Those who own their own distribution networks must constantly ask, What is the prime business? Am I a distributor who has a manufacturing facility or a manufacturer with my own distributors? Which is the profit center and which is the cost center?

Kresge took another approach. In the early 1960s when Kresge decided to enter the discount store business, it recognized that this business was different from its traditional variety store, requiring clothing, automotive equipment, sporting goods, other items that were outside Kresge's experience. But rather than starting out each department from scratch, Kresge leased space to businessmen who operated the department in K-Mart as though it was an independent store, paid K-Mart a percentage of the profits, and agreed to follow the discount thrust of K-Mart. Consumers did not know that these departments were separate businesses because they were so well integrated into the store and its motif. The lessees were knowledgeable, and they enabled K-Mart to offer products rapidly and still make a profit. Initially over 50% of K-Mart's sales were license-based. Within a few years, K-Mart began to acquire these lessees, and incorporate them in its own management. The lesson of this is clear: Instead of franchises, choose the licensing route.

Tandy Corporation has used a mixed approach to build its retail outlets. According to its 1977 annual report, Radio Shack grew worldwide, adding 1,400 owned stores and 1,350 dealers in four years, while reducing franchises.

SITUATION III: UNDIFFERENTIATED PRODUCT WHERE
VOLUME REALLY MATTERS

A third distribution-centered strategy is total saturation coverage. Normally this goes hand in hand with an aggressive "pull" strategy, but it can be the prime driver and the promotion can be a strong supporter. This approach has the advantage of making the intermediary—the dealer or distributor—a means and not an end, but it also minimizes the loyalty of both parties. It attracts opportunists who will support you only if you are the market leader but will desert you once you lose position or they can get a better deal elsewhere. Their desertion may hurt your reputation.

Distribution strategies require a management that is sales oriented and that has the ability to develop a strong personal and business relationship. You must determine which distributors match your product and business needs and carefully select them on the basis of those criteria. You must then decide how much control you wish to have and whether you want to have a long relationship with them or merely an opportunistic one.

If you require a lasting commitment, then you must track the distributor's performance and make sure that he is successful, that he is keeping up with trends, and that he is representing you properly. Relationships should be business oriented: If he is in trouble and is not performing well, then you must provide help—even financing, if that is needed. If he can't make it, you must decide either to acquire him or to just cut him off and seek another outlet. As a manager you must delegate the ongoing relationships, but you must be willing to get involved personally if necessary.

Service/Application-Directed Strategies

Thus far I have described strategies that try to identify and create customer needs from a product perspective. But there is an effective strategy whose aim is to provide service, which in turn increases the sale and use of the product. There are three service-based strategies that can be used separately or in combination: pre-sales service, application/use service, and repair and maintenance service. In this context, service is aimed at supporting the sale of the product or service, not merely to make a profit. In other words, the profit is to be made in the *product, not* in the service itself.

SITUATION I: COMPLEX PRODUCT, CONFUSED CUSTOMER

Many expensive, sophisticated products like computers, machinery, aircraft, and turbine generators require pre-sales support and even demonstrations, prototype development, and customization. In this case the product isn't sold because of the price, advertising, distributor, or manufacturing capacity, but precisely because of pre-sales service. The customer requires guidance in what to acquire and help in installing and operating the product. He may also need help in financing the purchase and in hiring and training people.

This strategic thrust is common in heavy-machinery-based industries, such as those that make and sell turbines, generators, motor, drives, controls, and so on. At times third parties are involved in this selection and specification by architectural engineers, but the supplier must still be involved and try to influence the decisions in his favor. In this case strong technical, financial, manufacturing, and engineering talents are needed to assure proper design and optimum performance.

In recent years a significant part of the service has been to assist the customer in getting government approval, especially in regulated industries. For instance, sales of nuclear power equipment depend on obtaining the approval of state agencies and of the Nuclear Regulatory Commission. The company with the ability to do this may be the winner, even if it is slightly more expensive. An article in *Fortune* pointed out that Burroughs was successful in banking because of the skills in applications selling that its salesmen possessed.*

* *Fortune,* January 1977.

SITUATION II: TRAINING THE USER
TO USE MORE

At times success depends on the ability to increase product usage. This is particularly true of products in which revenues are related to usage, not ownership. This is the case in a variety of industries, including computers, copy machines, electricity, telephones, and car rentals. (In fact, it is true of any rental business.)

The key, then, is to teach the customer how to use the equipment and then stimulate him to use it more and more. This has been the strategy of all the leaders in these industries. IBM has allocated a considerable amount of money to teaching customers how to apply the computer to all aspects of operating a business, from finance to inventory control, order processing, and engineering design—even to its use as a forecasting and decision-making tool. The company has even gone to the extent of developing complex software packages and providing them at little or no expense to the customer. Again, the strategy was aimed at selling and leasing and thereby at increasing usage.

Xerox has followed a similar strategy: Increase usage by providing education and trained consultants. Many years ago the large electrical power and distribution companies joined forces with utilities to increase usage. Part of this thrust was educational as well as promotional. Telephone service agents have increased business usage by increasing awareness and understanding of how to use the telephone as an effective communications tool.

This strategy requires trained professionals and educators. It is people-intensive and specifically requires people who understand how to provide service. The relationship doesn't end with the order and the invoice; it continues on a planned basis. Furthermore, the product design organization must be geared to developing equipment that can be used with minimum training and that can be supplemented by new, use-increasing features.

SITUATION III: CUSTOMER REQUIRES UTILIZATION
AND RELIABILITY

Many businesses require extremely high utilization and
can't afford to have their equipment break down. These are
normally capital-intensive businesses. For example, paper
mills are expensive to operate and suffer great economic
damage when they have equipment breakdowns. Therefore,
a paper company may be willing to pay a premium for the
product that is most reliable and whose supplier has a strong
readiness to repair it and to maintain it properly. This is
particularly true where unique repair and maintenance skills
are required and the customer can't obtain or afford his own.

This kind of service thrust has proved particularly effective in selling to offshore underdeveloped nations, but it has
also been important in Sears' appliance business. The critical
success factor in this area is the ability to respond quickly and
reliably to the customer. This requires the availability of spare
parts when they are needed and the ability to transport them
rapidly. In some cases it may require "standby" substitute
equipment like having a standby generator to install while the
customer's is being repaired.

The maintenance end requires good planning and quick
response to meet the customer's needs. Most companies and
individuals want to maintain when their business needs are
low or even when their plant is shut down for vacation. Of
course, responding to customer needs is the most critical factor of a service business, and you are likely to be most successful when you anticipate their needs and are able to respond
rapidly.

But at what point does the means become an end? When
do you stop driving the product via service and make it an
independent business or profit center? At some stage in the
product's life cycle the customer will learn to do the pre-sales
applications or repairs himself, and will become more interested in having the product priced *without* service. At the
same time, independents may enter the market to provide the

service separately, usually at a lower price. Thus, the service-driven strategy will become inappropriate, and management will be forced to select another. But it has an alternative—it can make the service a separate profit center and sell the service "unbundled" from the product. This is a good idea, but it must be carried out with planning and caution. You must always decide which is the highest priority—the product or the associated service. If you don't, you might lose both by antagonizing the customer.

Geographic/Segment Redefinition Strategy

The final marketing-based strategy I would like to discuss is the change in definition of the served market. This basically means that the management has decided to continue its manufacturing, pricing, orp romotional thrust, but to add or subs tract segments.

SITUATION I: GEOGRAPHIC MODIFICATION

At times a company decides to probe new geographic areas, be they foreign nations or different regions of the domestic market. It is most desirable for a company to be able to export its current product line without significant modifications. This can help increase volume with little or no addition to fixed assets, thus increasing overall profitability. This was the situation most American companies had in the early 1950s: European and Japanese markets were ripe for American imports, since demand was large and the indigenous manufacturers were still building capacity after the devastation of World War II. Thus, U.S. manufacturers moved into these markets with considerable ease and little resistance. Since American products were acceptable, there wasn't much of a need to change them, and profits were attractive. Today the situation is practically the reverse: The Europeans and Japanese are now moving aggressively to take an increasing share of the most attractive market in the world—the U.S. market. Japanese companies and their European counterparts are moving into the American market, first by importing their products directly and most recently by acquiring existing companies or by opening their own factories. For example, Fiat has moved into partnership with several U.S. companies, such as Allis-Fiat in the construction equipment market; Siemens joined with Allis-Chalmers to form a company to serve the American power generation equipment markets; Matsushita acquired Motorola's Quasar television business; Volkswagen, Sony, Datsun, and Toyota, as well as many German and Swiss chemical and drug manufacturers, have opened factories in the United States.

SITUATION II: SEGMENTATION/SCOPE CHANGE

But geographic expansion is only one side of the coin; there is also an opportunity to decrease scope and become more focused. (Nevertheless, as strange as it may seem, this option is difficult for management to accept.) It merely means that you should determine which areas bring in the highest profit margins, and then withdraw from those in which profits are lower. This can be accomplished by reducing or increasing the product offering or customer groupings. For instance, some companies decided to discontinue certain kinds of automobiles and concentrate on other kinds. This, of course, was the strategy of American Motors, which focused on the small car.

But there are other situations that illustrate the expansion of scope. For example, Sony started with the small-screen television primarily because its picture-tube configurations didn't meet the big-screen requirements. Gradually, however, as shown in Figure 4–1, the company has moved into the large-size screen, and now even offers a wide-screen set. Segmentation expansion can involve specific products, sizes, models, features, and accessories. It can also mean moving into various customer groupings—such as those who are price conscious—or even moving into original equipment manufacturing (OEM), wholesale, and retail sectors.

In the retail business there have been several illustrations of companies that have decided to change their traditional segmentation emphasis. For example, Carter Hawley Hale,

Figure 4-1. Sony's scope expansion, from small to large
television screen.

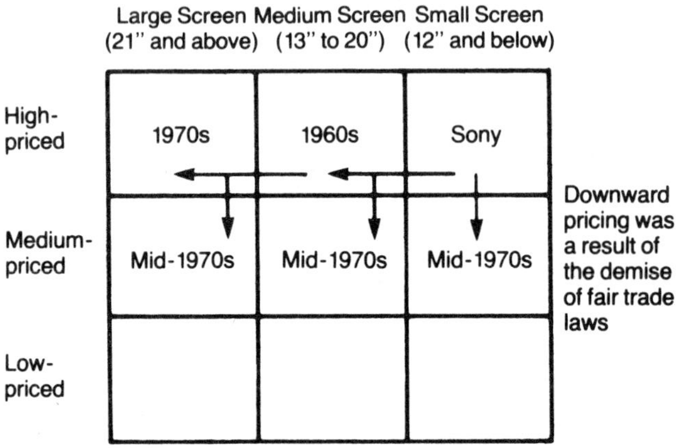

	Large Screen (21" and above)	Medium Screen (13" to 20")	Small Screen (12" and below)	
High-priced	1970s	1960s	Sony	Downward pricing was a result of the demise of fair trade laws
Medium-priced	Mid-1970s	Mid-1970s	Mid-1970s	
Low-priced				

the seventh largest department store chain in the United
States, decided to focus on the high-fashion segments and to
move from price/high-volume to high-margin segments. It
did this by acquiring store chains that had a reputation for
style, fashion, and exclusivity. The acquisitions included
Neiman Marcus, Bergdorf Goodman, and Canada's Holt,
Renfrew. Simultaneously, it upgraded the stock of its Broadway, Weinstock's Stores.* Sears had tried the same approach,
but with limited success.

   In an earlier section I pointed out that Texas Instruments
normally used learning curve pricing to enter and lead a
market. Its entry into citizens band radio, however, was quite
different. In this case it moved into the top end of the line and
emphasized high prices and innovative product, rather than
fighting it out with its price-oriented competitors.† In addition, Rockwell Microelectronics decided to move from the
mass to the custom IC chip segment.

* *Fortune,* December 1976.
† *Business Week,* May 23, 1977.

Critical Success Factors

The critical factors required to expand and contract either geographic or segment participation include, first of all, adaptability and a willingness to meet the new geographic or segment requirements. For example, if you decide to move into a new geographic area, such as the Middle East, you must be willing to supply a product that fits this region's needs and to conform to the business conditions and requirements of that area. As the saying goes, "When in Rome. . . ." This is probably the most critical aspect of moving into a new product segment as well: You don't sell a Volkswagen in the same way that you sell a Mercedes, and you don't move into a small-volume segment with a high-volume facility. You don't service a retailer in the same way that you service an OEM.

On the contraction (and expansion) side, the most important aspect is objectivity and the willingness to follow through with your plans. You must carefully evaluate all the segments or regions that you serve and, if several of them don't meet your expectations, you should be willing to discontinue your participation. Furthermore, once you make your decision, follow through and don't be ambivalent. This only confuses the customers, and when customers are confused, they may buy from someone else, which could mean that you will lose the segment anyway, but possibly at a loss instead of at a profit.

Matching Marketing-Based Strategies with Investment Strategies

Thus, you can see that there are many marketing-based options available to management, whether your investment strategy emphasizes sales, profit, or cash growth. But before I complete this discussion, let me outline which marketing strategies fit the various investment options available to you. (See Table 4–1 for a concise review of all the marketing-based strategies I discussed.)

Penetration Strategies

Any of the marketing-based strategies can help you penetrate a market. Identification of needs and wants can be used either to create new markets or to increase your share in existing markets. Demand creation by advertising or pricing is also appropriate to this aggressive strategy. With a penetration strategy, distribution can be increased along with geographic and segment expansion. Service, particularly preselling, can be used to increase the size and share of the market.

Hold-and-Defend and Harvesting Strategies

Identifying your customers' needs and wants and maintaining their awareness of your product and service are essential to any hold-and-defend strategy, as is promoting brand identification by advertising. Pricing can be extremely useful in holding and defending a position or share. If you reduce prices, you can make it very expensive for someone to gain share and, at the same time, you will keep the customer loyal to your product. But pricing is a delicate tool and must be handled in such a way as to prevent an open and possibly deadly price war.

Distribution can also be used to prevent inroads. This requires dealer loyalty and emphasis on the best, most critical dealers. If you concentrate your effort on the most profitable geographic areas and segments, you will be able to hold share and protect your position. Providing good service is yet another effective technique to maintain customer loyalty.

Reduction-of-Share Strategies

Harvesting has fewer marketing-based options. Applications aimed at customer needs and wants, as well as at demand creation, are not that useful in harvesting a business, since they may require more inflow of capital and cash than a harvesting approach may warrant.

Pricing is a practical approach to reduction of share and even to the slowing of growth. This is commonly called "selling off share," and is used quite often (but possibly more unconsciously than deliberately). The same approach is used in distribution-, geographic-, and service-driven thrusts. In each case you are either cutting back product availability and service or making the customers pay extra if they want the product badly enough. The problem is one of execution: If the price is too high or the availability poor, it may provide an umbrella under which an aggressive competitor can sneak into the market and gain share. (An umbrella price is one set high enough by the industry leader to permit the higher cost competitors to participate at a profit. In other words, it holds a protective umbrella over their heads.) Thus, if handled badly, a harvest may become a steep decline, forcing premature exit or divestment.

Exit/Divestment Strategies

Exit strategies are restricted to pricing, distribution, geographic contraction, and elimination of service. The major difference between harvesting and exit is one of degree and timing. In the latter case, you want to get out with a minimum of investment and a maximum of profit.

Divestment strategies may require some investment and can include the use of advertising, price, distribution, and geographic approaches to make the business appear to be healthy and an attractive purchase. Again, the key is careful management and execution, since you wish to invest only what it takes to make the business attractive to potential purchasers. If you invest too much, you will reduce your return; if you invest too little, you may reduce the value of the business and possibly the number of those interested in purchasing it.

Table 4–1 (on the following pages) summarizes the marketing-based strategies discussed in this chapter.

Table 4–1.

Type	Situation	Critical Success Factors
Need/Want identification	Leader recognizes need for improving product New entry surfaces unaddressed need	Customer can recognize need Market research Product planning Patience and willingness and ability to sustain losses Opportunity for customer to learn at minimum risk Strong integration
Demand-creating	Building brand image Share gain in stable market Maintaining balance of power	Product satisfaction Media selection Readiness to serve Understanding management
Pricing *High*	Quality image Supply limited Monopolistic/proprietary product	Perceived value of product Customer satisfaction Control of dealers Warranties
Low	Volume Buying share Learning curve impact	Least cost position Minimum overhead Risk acceptance

Summary of marketing-based strategies.

Type	*Situation*	*Critical Success Factors*
Distribution	Unique product/weak finances Unique brand acceptance Undifferentiated with high volume needs	Selection/control of distributors Ability to improve effectiveness and efficiency of distributors and dealers
Service	Complex product/ confused customer Increased usage Customer requires utilization and reliability	Ability to instruct Forecasting of needs User-oriented decisions Spare parts Diagnostics Standby and back-up equipment Recognition of means vs. end
Geographic/ segment	Geographic modification Desired scope change	Insight on differences—between new and existing segments or regions Willingness to substitute segments

5

Production-Based
Strategies

AS I was researching this book, I was struck by the lack of
highly visible, well-publicized production- and manufac-
turing-driven strategies, although popular business magazines, case studies, and even investment analysts' reports had
numerous illustrations of companies that have grown and
have defended their positions through the use of creative
marketing strategies and innovative products and services. As
I considered this situation, I concluded that manufacturing
strategies, although common and effective, are often taken
for granted and are not given sufficient publicity.

There are a number of production-led strategies that I
would like to describe and illustrate, including:

1. *Capacity*-based strategies, the use of capacity to gain
   both a market and cost advantage.

2. *Innovative* and *proprietary* equipment-, processes-, and systems-driven strategies.
3. *Efficiency*-oriented strategies, which provide the opportunity to aggressively develop new markets or to reap the rewards of increased profitability.
4. *Supply-assurance* strategies aimed at increasing confidence in the availability of supply.
5. *Deployment* and *readiness-to-serve* strategies, which provide competitive advantage in being able to respond rapidly to customer strategies.

I have not listed a cost strategy here, since I believe that cost is a result of these or other strategies. As in previous chapters, I shall identify situations that illustrate the strategy I am discussing.

Capacity-Based Strategies

Long-Cycle, Capital-Intensive Markets

A number of industries require several years and hundreds of millions of dollars to build capacity. For instance, it takes five to seven years and more than $250 million to build a paper mill. The same is true of chemical plants, refineries, and power generation facilities, whose time and cost of construction have been extended even further with the increased number of state and local ordinances and the need to get environmental control approval and to engage in court fights. This situation provides an excellent opportunity for a "risk-taking" and financially strong company to invest in a new capacity well in advance of demand. If properly planned, the capacity will be available just at the time that the demand materializes, and the company will thereby have an excellent competitive position. This strategy was employed by both Weyerhauser and Union Camp, who had the foresight to build plants and add capacity when the rest of the industry was reluctant to invest.

This strategy requires good forecasting ability and sound data on current capacity situation. If the demand forecast is too optimistic, the company may have excess capacity and thereby add to an already serious problem of overcapacity, which may in turn result in all of the competitors' being willing to cut prices merely to fill the plant—an unprofitable situation for all. A second requirement is the ability to predict a competitor's reaction. If the industry has a "herd" mentality—namely, that everyone follows the leader—then each competitor will add capacity, thus resulting in overcapacity for everyone at a later period. Finally, financing is critical: The company should be neither overextended nor overoptimistic about getting financing at a later date.

High Breakeven Points

High-fixed-costs industries normally have high breakeven points. Some plants require a minimum of 92% utilization to operate profitably; anything over 95% is extremely profitable. Thus, many companies have a capacity utilization strategy, which they synchronize carefully with pricing actions. When business is good and the plant is already filled, prices and terms are kept high and promises on delivery are extended. This was the situation in the early 1970s, when paper and packaging materials were in scarce supply. (You may recall that at that time, paper producers had record earnings.) When capacity utilization dips below the breakeven point, then the company aggressively seeks new business to fill the plant through price, extended terms of payment, added services, or a decision to withdraw capacity rather than take on unprofitable business. The latter strategy was carried out by several paper companies in the mid-1970s when they elected to close down mills rather than reduce prices.

Business Week * reported on the impact of low-capacity utilization on Japan. The Japanese were faced with a declining home market resulting from consumers' reluctance to buy and from an increase in savings. This consumer reaction resulted in a considerable level of underutilization, decreased profits, and a 19% increase in bankruptcies. The Japanese

* October 24, 1977.

responded by dramatically increasing exports to the United States, thereby causing price pressures and lower profits among American companies. Thus, capacity utilization can be used to increase sales or to maintain income. In some instances a company may take on business that exceeds the theoretical level of 100% of capacity. This can be done because capacity is calculated to include time for normal repairs and maintenance. In the situation in which utilization exceeds 100%, the company runs the plant at that level for extended periods of time without performing the necessary maintenance. This results in large earnings, but could sacrifice the long term for the short run. It is an excellent harvesting alternative. This strategy requires the ability to know the optimum level of utilization precisely and to know how to track and monitor costs. Furthermore, you must know when to back off: This is particularly true when industry capacity exceeds demand. The worst situation is when a competitor gets desperate and takes irrational actions, such as assuming long-term commitments at a loss. This sounds impossible, but it has happened, and it causes everyone to suffer in the long run. Utilization strategies require the development and careful execution of contingency plans.

Process/Equipment Innovation-Driven Strategies

Unique Know-How

Many industries require unique know-how and skills and specially designed equipment. This is true in the chemical, pharmaceutical, cosmetics, and glass industries. The ingredients are known, but precisely how they are mixed, at what temperature, and under what specific conditions, will make the difference between success and failure. This is especially true when product patents expire. It is like making bread— you need to know the critical steps and timing: If you put the yeast in too soon or cook the bread too long, it won't turn out correctly. Until recently, many products didn't list the ingredients and kept their formulas top secret. Some companies design and develop their own unique equipment and systems to give them a competitive advantage. The end product may be a commodity, but the competitors may not replicate the exact characteristics. In fact, the equipment rather than the product may be patented. This is the situation in the manufacture of light bulbs, plastics, metal containers, and synthetics.

Thus, process innovation can be used to lead or to protect and defend your position. Unique processes can be used to support productivity and efficiency thrusts: They may help you increase material yields or possibly achieve quality levels not available to your competition. At times this requires development and installation of new, expensive equipment. For instance, the development of complex VLSI (very large-scale integration) semiconductors has led to installation of complex equipment, which has raised the cost of participating in this industry. At one time a small company could enter the semiconductor business for less than $1 million; this has increased by five to ten times over the past few years. *Business Week* * reported that Japan and West Germany have invested hundreds of millions of dollars to promote VLSI projects.

Increasing numbers of companies have been forced to change their strategies from market- and product-based to production-focused strategies, because of the need to comply with government regulations or with environmental and pollution standards. New systems have been developed to comply with the rules and, although capital expenditures have increased, the companies have been able to stay in the business, and they continue to compete.

Thus, process improvement and automation have many rewards, but they also have certain conditions that must be met. First of all, processes and systems must be customized to fit the manufacturer's needs, and this requires knowledge of the product and of the total manufacturing system—"off the shelf" approaches won't provide the competitive barrier required. Second, the process must meet customers' requirements and not force them to change. (The customer is buying a specific product or function and doesn't really care how the

* Ibid.

product was made.) This requires constant surveillance, both of customer needs and of manufacturing fit. If the customer's needs and expectations change, then the process must respond.

To be sure that the process you have selected hasn't lost its competitive edge, you must study other approaches as well. Finally, the company must be willing to continue to invest. This is graphically demonstrated by many of America's metal industries, particularly the steel industry, which wasn't willing to spend the money on keeping its process lead. The Japanese, on the other hand, did invest, and in early 1977 it was reported that they were able to produce, ship, and sell steel profitably at a price lower than the American steel maker could. As the old saying goes, "Some industries must invest heavily just to stay even."

Another illustration of this principle occurred in the paper industry when Weyerhauser installed a thermomechanical pulp mill that used a process developed by Sweden's Defibrator. This new process enabled Weyerhauser to conserve new materials, make stronger paper, and reduce the workforce by 45%.

Transportable Factories

There are several other ingenious illustrations of new manufacturing approaches that have become the foundations of new strategies. One deals with the manufacture of Kayakas in a trailer van and another with the use of ships as factories. *Business Week* * reported that a company called Arcouettes developed a manufacturing process to make Kayakas in a trailer. This approach looked so promising because shipping Kayakas by interstate commercial trucks is very expensive. However, by the use of a rotational molding approach, the trailer can be transported to the retailer's or dealer's location and the Kayakas can be manufactured to order right on site. This innovation could be just as powerful a means of creating a competitive barrier as an entirely unique product would be. Of course, it has limitations as well: What would happen if the

* May 23, 1977.

trailer were damaged in transit? It could destroy the entire
company! There have been several illustrations of factories being
built on ships. The Japanese, who are among the leaders in
transport ships, have used ships as factories. *Business Week* *
pointed out that a ship was being converted by the Japanese
into a Kraft paper mill and power plant, that others were
being planned for use as 2,000-ton-per-day floating desalina-
tion plants for Saudi Arabia, and that another was being designed for prefabricated home construction. The merits of
these approaches is that they provide a means to utilize
Japanese ships while creating a total productive system.

This shows that a strategy can be based on a need outside
the specific business situation, but that there can be advantages to this approach nevertheless. First of all, a portable
factory can sail to the least expensive port and use the low-cost
labor there. Furthermore, it can build enough product to
satisfy a small economy, store it, then sail to another location
and return later when the supply declines. A few years ago,
Westinghouse proposed construction of nuclear power plants
offshore. The potential benefit of such a project was to cir-
cumvent the delays and restrictions caused by environmen-
talists. Westinghouse formed a joint venture with Tenneco to
build these plants and it even obtained orders, but unfortunately its timing was bad, since the nuclear business came to a
virtual halt, and the joint-venture company was dismantled.

Manufacturing Efficiency- and Productivity-Based Strategies

Many corporate executive officers base their strategies
purely on efficiency and productivity. This often results in
their becoming the "least-cost producers." This strategy
should permeate the entire organization, not just manufacturing. It is really simple—it relies on strong controls, decisive
management, and timely information, all of which result in

* August 15, 1977.

high product turnover and low inventory and overhead. Let us consider a few examples.

Under Gen. David Sarnoff, RCA was reputed to be a technological innovator, having almost singlehandedly developed the color television business through its development of the color receiver, the picture camera, and color television programming. However, Robert Sarnoff, the general's son, aimed at diversification, moving the company into computers, furniture, foods, and many other product areas. He wasn't successful and he resigned under pressure when he was forced to liquidate and suffer losses on computers. Today RCA is headed by a veteran and pragmatist, Ed Griffiths. Mr. Griffiths' strategy is aimed at emphasizing short-term earnings through efficiency, productivity, and tough controls. Mr. Griffiths was willing to abort the video disc venture if it didn't appear to have a potential for high and immediate profitability, even though millions of dollars have already been spent on its development. Although Griffiths' strategy may have made sense in the short run, it could have been a danger to RCA, especially in light of the long-range threat of Japanese and European technology-based companies.

Petrie Shops, which is in the women's wear business, has a strategy based on tight controls that are aimed at increasing turnover and profits. The shops focus only on teenagers and slender older women. They are based in shopping centers, sell only for cash, provide no delivery or alterations, do no advertising, and sell only unbranded merchandise. If goods don't sell, they are rapidly marked down to increase turnover (13.5 turns, or times a product is sold in a given period, normally a year). This strategy is based on nothing exotic—just good, sound, tough, focused management.

By building on stringent fiscal and manufacturing controls, Emerson Electric has led the way in sales and profitability growth. It uses an "ABC" budgeting system, which requires managers to have three plans—the "A" plan is the negotiated budget plan, the "B" is for 10% less, and the "C" is for a 20% less contingency. Managers' rewards are closely tied to these measures. To maintain a high level of productivity,

Emerson aggressively fights the union, and it prefers small plants to large ones.

In every case I identified, the critical factor for success seems to be the chief executive officer. The CEO must be disciplined and decisive: He or she isn't a visionary, but a pragmatist, and he is dedicated to winning. This dedication is translated into profits. In addition, the CEO has to be backed up by a strong financial control system that measures productivity and quickly surfaces deviations. Nonunion status also seems to be a strong asset because it permits greater flexibility.

Supply-Assurance Strategies

In the mid-1970s, the developed nations of the world awoke to the terrifying reality that their industrial capabilities were dependent on the underdeveloped nations. Although it was always recognized that the sources of critical minerals and metals—copper, petroleum, platinum, tin, diamonds—were in these nations, no one predicted the ability of these countries to control the availability and price of the critical commodities. This was the greatest shock since the Japanese and Germans cut off the supply of critical materials during World War II.

These events have caused many companies to initiate supply-based strategies, and I would like to discuss five of them in particular:

1. Material reduction or substitution.
2. Long-term commitments.
3. Backward integration via ownership.
4. Joint development.
5. Sourcing-based strategies.

Reducing the Amount of Materials

In this strategy, an excessive amount of human and financial resources is applied to the reduction of material content. For instance, the sizes of automobiles have been greatly reduced—not merely to reduce the amount of metal in them but also to reduce the amount of gasoline required to run them. This was a result of governmental regulations that forced automobile companies to reduce gasoline consumption. Many paper companies have reduced their pulp requirements by using recycled paper instead of virgin fibers. Du Pont has many projects that are aimed at reducing costs and the amount of materials in the manufacturing processes. The company has allocated 78% of its R&D funds in 1978 to this kind of development. For instance, it is working on a new process that makes the intermediate product used in the manufacture of nylon and that could cut over $60 million in the company's manufacturing costs. Another project aims at reducing the silver content of photographic film by 10%, resulting in millions of dollars in savings.

SUBSTITUTING NEW MATERIALS

In addition to merely reducing the amount of materials, many companies have undertaken extensive product and process redesign to use entirely new materials. As the cost and availability of natural fibers changed, many clothing, furniture, and rug companies used synthetics as substitutes for natural fibers. For instance, most rugs sold today use nylon or rayon rather than wool. Furthermore, most clothing is made of these synthetics instead of cotton and wool, and vinyls have replaced silks and satins on upholstered furniture. Companies have used these substitutes as a means of unseating the market leader. The same is true of automobiles: Components have increasingly been made of plastics rather than of steel, chrome, or aluminum. This trend is expected to continue and even to intensify, again driven by the need to reduce weight in cars so as to increase gasoline mileage.

This strategy can be enhanced by the engineering and manufacturing staffs' use of "value engineering.' This technique was developed in the early 1950s to reduce costs. It tears products apart and analyzes each component to determine the criticality of the function performed and the cost of providing the function. The engineering staff then determines whether the function is really necessary or if it could be done differently at a lower cost. In a way this is the engineer's version of "zero-based budgeting": Nothing is taken for granted and everything is analyzed from a cost and functional need basis. If the component isn't needed, it is removed; if the process can be performed more cheaply by using another material, then it is redesigned.

Making Long-Term Commitments

But suppose that a material is absolutely critical and that you can neither reduce its use nor substitute for it in your production process. Then you may have to make an aggressive move to obtain either long-term contracts or a partial or total equity position.

First of all, you can sign long-term contracts with suppliers. These contracts may assure you a given supply at a specified price. Many companies tried this approach, but the contracts proved practically worthless when the going got rough. This was particularly true when the suppliers were nationalized or were taken over by other companies.

There were many petroleum companies whose strategy called for depending on others for their feedstock. This worked well when there was an abundant supply but was almost a disaster when the supply became limited. A large number of Midwestern manufacturers decided to switch from oil and coal to natural gas because it was cheaper. During the energy crisis these companies suddenly found that the supply of natural gas had become scarce, and in some cases they were forced to cut back on production and even close their plants. The story has been periodically repeated whenever a manufacturer has become overly dependent on a mineral or material like tin, copper, uranium, diamonds, and platinum. Long-range contractually based supply strategies may be less capital-intensive but certainly risky when supply shortages occur.

Backward Integration

As a result, many companies have decided upon backward integration, going back as far as the source of materials. Of course, this isn't new: For years the major oil companies have integrated backward, have owned and controlled refineries and drilling equipment, and have even provided the manpower and financing to do the exploration. The "Seven Sisters" were completely integrated from oil field to service station. General Motors has also integrated backward to assure the availability and low cost of needed components. This is quite normal when a company is large enough to use the majority of its supplies effectively and when the market has matured to the point at which cost reduction can be readily translated into profits. That was when GM acquired Fisher bodies, shock companies, spark plug companies, and so on.

Fortune * described how Dow Chemical instituted a comprehensive supply-based strategy to give it greater access to raw materials and energy than its competitors. Today Dow can supply 15% of its own natural gas supply, it has an interest in a "gathering company" to provide an additional 35%, and the remainder is covered under long-term contracts. It is capable of providing 200,000 barrels of crude oil a day, and has invested in equipment and facilities to convert liquefied petroleum into naphtha. Eighty percent of its electrical needs is supplied by its own generators, and it is working on a new gasified lignite process. In short, Dow Chemical is attempting to create a competitive barrier by having a guaranteed, relatively low-cost source of critical raw materials and energy.

The prime reason that this strategy makes sense is the concern about availability and cost. This is especially true when the source of supply lies thousands of miles away and is in the hands of a sheikh, monarch, Communist state, or dictatorship: Even if these countries are currently friendly, they may not be so in the future. Governments can be overthrown, or leaders may suddenly decide to use their supply for political or economic purposes. The revolution in Iran shows the unpredictability and suddenness of a change of this sort. But owning your own supply can have economic advantages as well: Mining and exploration provide tax advantages, since they can be used to defer income or accelerate depreciations, and the sale of by-products can be very profitable, too.

As you can see, backward integration can be an excellent way of increasing profits by reducing costs; it can also help assure supply during times of scarcity. But this approach has its limitations, especially in rapidly changing or growing mar-

* May 1977.

kets: It may cause the leader to resist changes because they are too expensive and the leader thinks that he has too much to lose. As a result, a more flexible, nonintegrated company may move in and obtain a foothold. In this case, integration can reduce flexibility.

Joint Development

But ownership isn't the only viable way of assuring supply. In recent years oil companies have found exploration too expensive to undertake on their own, and so they now use joint-development approaches. This usually takes the form of jointly owned exploration companies. Other kinds of firms have formed joint companies to develop substitute materials. (This approach has become very popular in Europe and Japan.) For example, in the United States, many electric utilities have joined together to purchase and store uranium for nuclear power plants. In October 1977, Continental Oil and Monsanto formed a joint venture to manufacture ethylene and to process crude oil into feedstock for their use. Alcan Aluminum, Royal Dutch Shell, and ARCO developed a jointly owned company to build a $500 million aluminum plant in Ireland.

Sourcing-Based Strategies

About a decade ago, it became painfully obvious to many American companies that the Japanese had won the consumer electronics race. As a result, many American electronics companies decided to stop making products of their own. But rather than leave the business, these companies contracted with manufacturers in the Far East to make products to *their* specifications, so that they had their "own" product without actually manufacturing it. This was the strategy adopted by companies like Lloyds, Soundesign, and Electrophonics in the radio and stereophonic market and by all U.S. television manufacturers in the videotape recorder market.

This strategy isn't new; it has been used by Sears for decades. In the 1930s, Sears decided that it wanted to have its own brand rather than carry national brands. So it worked out long-term contracts with many manufacturers to provide completed products, made to Sears's specifications and using Sears's brands, such as Coldspot and Kenmore. This has been a very successful strategy and, although it has been attempted by other retailers, only Sears has made it work. Sears hasn't attempted to fully integrate backward, although at times it has assumed partial ownership in several of its vendors. This equity, however, may have stemmed from the vendors' need for cash, rather than from any desire on Sears's part to own vendors.

Sourcing-based strategies enable a company to participate in markets for which it doesn't have the critical manufacturing skills and know-how but for which it does have the proper marketing and distribution skills. Such a strategy can provide a means of opportunistically participating in a market, but the danger is that the source of supply may stop selling, and consequently you will be left without a product. Sears has had to face this problem many times: In some situations, it was able to obtain an alternative product; in other cases, it purchased the vendor and finally discontinued the line or used national brand merchandise.

Many wholesale appliance distributors who handled Philco appliances were faced with the same problem. When Ford acquired Philco in the late 1950s to compete with GM's Frigidaire, the company invested considerable financial resources to make Philco a winner, but it was ultimately unsuccessful. Its last attempt was to offer a line of energy-conserving appliances, but the public wasn't willing to pay the premium. Subsequently, Philco announced that it was exiting the business, thereby leaving its distributors without a refrigerator line. Since General Electric and Frigidaire both sold directly through company-owned distribution and the other major producers already had independent wholesalers, these distributors were faced with a choice—get a new product line or quit.

The distributors decided to band together and form a buying pool to obtain a private-label line. Since the Crosley brand was defunct, they decided to reintroduce this line and to have it built to their specifications by other manufacturers.

Rockwell/Admiral would provide the refrigerator line; Revco would make freezers; Hardwick, gas and electric ranges; and McGraw-Edison, air conditioners. Sourcing products actually enabled these wholesalers to survive and to compete effectively against the national brands, but it is still unclear whether this strategy will be successful.

Successfully Carrying Out Supply-Assurance Strategies

Supply-assurance strategies require unique skills, knowhow, and management. First of all, managers should understand the problems of *all* aspects of a backward-integrated business and, if necessary, they should hire experts in all specific areas of the enterprise to be sure that the business is properly managed at the lowest possible cost. It makes no sense to have a captive supply that costs more than the same minerals or metals would cost if they were obtained from another source. This means efficient production and a proper level of investment to keep the costs low. Second, both the risks and the rewards must be properly assessed. Too many managers think about the rewards and forget the risks involved in an undertaking.

In Chile, Argentina, and the Mideast many companies have their own mines and have built refineries and converting facilities only to see these facilities expropriated by the host government. This is a major risk and should always be considered in deciding on backward integration. Other risks that can outweigh the advantages of ownership include a prolonged and even destructive strike and accelerated costs of extracting the mineral, shipping it, and installing special environmental or safety equipment. Building the entire business around a single source of supply, even if it is company owned and operated, may turn out to be a major problem.

Third, the long-term supply situation must be properly evaluated. If you are going to invest in a material that will be replaced by another mineral or synthetic in the near future, then it makes little sense to make the investment.

Fourth, if you intend to own foreign properties, you must be able to deal with the host government. This may include the ability to negotiate or to quickly liquidate your holdings.

Your success may depend on your knowledge of and skills in doing business in the foreign environment, and it requires great tact and sensitivity.

Fifth, knowledge of total logistical systems may be critical. The Japanese have taught us how to deal with a shortage situation. We all know that the Japanese have few resources of their own: They import petroleum, iron ore, and most other valuable minerals. To cope with this problem, they built a fleet of vessels that are used to export goods as well as to carry minerals, so that today Japan has one of the largest merchant fleets in the world. This shows that without a *total* system, backward integration may be economically unsound.

Deployment and Readiness-to-Serve Management Strategies

A deployment strategy is based on the ability to be truly responsive to the customer's need for rapid or firm delivery. If he needs it in two weeks, overnight, or on July 9, he must get it with no excuses and a 100% assurance level. This, too, is a hybrid strategy and is dependent on responsive sales and manufacturing organizations. It may be the only way to assure customer loyalty and to prevent price erosion. It is particularly applicable to commodity products and key components of a larger system.

This strategy requires both a willingness to keep large stocks of certain materials and a systematic delivery approach. It may require large inventories and cash tied up in inventory, as well as extensive warehousing and shipping equipment. In today's competitive climate you must be willing to invest in data processing systems that carefully record your inventory levels and the timing of deliveries. This is similar to computers that help oil companies decide when to deliver their oil. The major risk here is that the system is inaccurate and you may wind up with too much, too little, or the wrong mix of inventory.

This strategy has become the driver behind the growth of wholesalers who serve hardware and home improvement centers and auto parts dealers. In this case, entirely new organizations have grown up and taken share from the less efficient

Table 5–1.

Type	Situation
Capacity—advance	Long-cycle, capital-intensive markets
Capacity—utilization	High breakeven point
Process/equipment innovation	Required by industry Building a barrier Governmental regulations
Manufacturing efficiency and productivity	Need to be "least or lowest cost" producer

Supply assurance
Substitution
Backward integration
	Reduction/substitution
	New materials—a substitute
	Backward integration
	Source product
	  Cost
	  Scarcity
	  Competitive advantage

Deployment and readiness to serve	Competitive advantage of speed and accuracy Advantage to "open stock"

Summary of production-based strategies.

Relative Position	Critical Success Factors
Risk-taking Financially strong	Good forecasting Ability to anticipate competitors' reactions Financing ability Willingness to assume risks
Low utilization	Knowledge of optimum level of utilization Ability to monitor costs Plan and willingness to back off (contingency planning)
Internal ability to innovate and finance	Ability to customize Recognition that process won't force customer to change Surveillance of other approaches Long-term investment commitment
Strong cost position	Strong CEO Strong controls Decisive management Timely information
Strong leadership position Strong financial position	Understanding of materials business Ability to assess risks and rewards Supply forecasting Dealing with foreign countries Total logistical system and know-how Timely information
Strong distribution Strong financial position	Large stocks of critical items Systematic delivery Timely and current information systems Cash flow to sustain

wholesalers or manufacturers, because these new firms have developed a stronger readiness-to-serve capability. The same kind of strategy has been used by service companies in consumer, commercial, and industrial sectors. For instance, the repair of appliances has been enhanced by the use of radio-dispatched, well-stocked repair trucks to fix televisions, refrigerators, and ranges. Again, premium prices are charged because of the ability to fix rapidly and accurately.

Another form of this strategy is the open-stock policy of some furniture and china manufacturers, like Ethan Allen and Lenox. Both of these companies assure the consumer that they can replace or add to the furniture or dinnerware at a later date. This is very valuable in markets where the product is expensive or the customer doesn't have the space. For instance, good china or sterling silver is expensive, and the family may wish to add to the set at a later date, or the family may have a small house and wish to add to their furniture set at a later date. This is another form of readiness to serve.

Conclusion

Although marketing strategies have been given considerable publicity, manufacturing-focused strategies can be equally effective in penetrating new markets, defending positions, or even gradually harvesting. (For a summary of production-based strategies, their uses, and critical success factors, see Table 5–1.) You can add capacity in advance of demand, create a unique process, or even tie up a valuable resource in advance of demand to gain share. Furthermore, an efficient manufacturing process plus high capacity utilization or low-cost supply can move a company into a highly profitable but defendable position. Finally, by limiting investment in new capacity or warehousing or sale of supplies, a company can gradually harvest or even profitably exit from a business.

Of course, the total plan must be properly integrated with other business and functional strategies. This will be discussed further in Chapter 8.

6

Innovation:
The Glamour Strategy

IN the previous two chapters, I described how marketing-
and production-driven strategies can enable a company to
gain share, increase volume, hold or defend a market, or even
gradually give up share. These strategies emphasize how the
product is *sold* or *produced*, not changing the product itself.

But there are times when more drastic actions are required and when growth or defense necessitates a radically
different or considerably modified product. This is where innovation comes in. Innovation is based on the recognition
that the customer and market are ready for a new way to
perform a task or to meet a specific need. The innovator
provides the "better way." The product innovator looks at a
situation—such as one in which consumers seek an efficient,
abundant, and less expensive way of heating and cooling their
homes and offices—and will consider new ways of providing
this function. Consumers don't really care whether their heat

is provided by sun, oil, gas, wood, or electricity; they just want to be heated or cooled, and will accept the best means available.

Product innovation may also be the result of an invention developed without consideration for the user, and it must then be sold. This is what I call a "product looking for a market." It occurs because an inventor has an interest in a specific scientific or creative area.

Innovation-based strategies are glamorous and there are hundreds of successful illustrations of them, but we never hear about the thousands of failures. This strategy has high rewards, but equally high risks. Quite often the difference is a direct result of timing: If the innovator introduces the product or service too soon—before the customer recognizes the need for it—and if the innovator doesn't have sufficient financial resources to stimulate the customer's recognition of the need or to wait until it matures naturally, then the project will fail. Many of today's products were invented decades ago. Air conditioners were invented in the early 1900s, but they didn't become popular until the 1950s, and even today they don't have a high saturation. The electric lamp was invented in 1879, but it took over 35 years to be sold in sufficient quantities to make a profit.

If a company improves on its best-selling product, it may hurt itself, since the customers may decide to stop buying the current product, thus reducing the company's overall sales and profitability. On the other hand, if the company waits too long to innovate, it may lose its lead and find itself unable to catch up. Kodak, for example, was not interested in instant photography because it thought that that process would substitute for its own popular-selling camera. Furthermore, instant photography didn't require film development, which was a significant market for Kodak. Thus, Kodak permitted Polaroid to gain a strong position and, even when it finally decided to enter this market, Kodak had an extremely difficult time competing with Polaroid, which already had a commanding position.

In this chapter I would like to discuss three basic strategic options and some variations on each. Every company must decide whether it wishes to be a leader, a quick follower, or a slow follower, or not to follow at all in its key markets. Furthermore, it must decide whether the "leader" or "follower" strategies that it chooses will be self-generated or will require the innovations of others.

The Leadership Role

There are a number of reasons that a business executive may choose to become the innovative leader. These reasons include:

— The desire to prevent a product or segment from maturing too quickly.
— The desire to discourage the competition from being too aggressive.
— The desire to "leap frog" the current leader and change the factors for success.
— The desire to have the industry standardized in order to sell accessories, services, and spare parts.
— The need to respond to legislation, regulation, and environmentally created opportunities.

SITUATION I: MARKET LEADER WISHES TO EXTEND THE LIFE OF A MATURING PRODUCT

We all know that products and markets pass through stages of life from conception to childhood to adulthood and then to old age. This cycle will vary in length, depending on the product: Some consumer products pass from the beginning to the end of the cycle in a few years, whereas industrial products may take decades. The life cycle plots volume against time, as is illustrated in Figure 6–1.

But there are also strategies that can extend this cycle considerably. One strategy involves adding new features or performance characteristics that renew customers' interest and may even entice them to replace their current products

Figure 6-1. The life cycle of a product, from youth to old age.

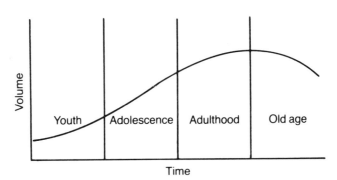

Figure 6-2. Extending a product's life span through innovation.

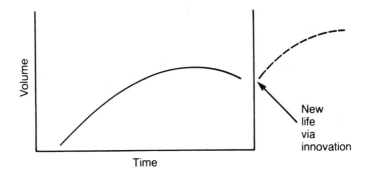

with yours at an earlier date. This strategy is depicted in Figure 6-2.

The need to invest in innovation to extend market or product life is often difficult for a market leader to comprehend and implement. The reasons are understandable: The market leader is making better than average profits, and life is easy for him—"Why change?" he asks. But the smart and consistent winners overcome their complacency and invest in the future rather than in the present.

The strategy of innovating to extend product life has been

successfully implemented by many consumer and industrial companies. For example, General Motors invented the annual or semiannual model change. This was a combination of new styling and the addition of exciting new features, each designed to create consumer interest. Model changes caused dissatisfaction with current models, even when the automobiles still had considerable useful life in them. This strategy forced Ford to follow, and it has contributed to the sale of millions of automobiles each year. Imagine how many cars would have been sold if the automobile industry had followed Henry Ford's standardized one-color strategy! There would be fewer new cars on the road, and industry sales would be considerably lower. Furthermore, competition would be based more on price than on features and innovations.

This feature improvement strategy has been followed in other consumer areas as well. General Electric has added a number of features to refrigerators to develop market growth. These features have included automatic defrosting; automatic ice-making; through-door ice water, beverages, and ice cubes; and decorative colors for refrigerators. In cooking ranges, GE has innovated by providing self-cleaning ovens and microwave cooking features. RCA innovated in television by improving controls and by introducing color television.

Today, a number of companies are using computers and microprocesses to add to a whole array of products. Amana used a microcomputer to increase the use of microwave ovens. New controls have been added to machine tools to increase their precision, flexibility, and ease of operation. These new features have enhanced the attractiveness of the new products and have stimulated replacement sales.

At times environmental forces stimulate demand for new features. In the 1970s, there has been a growing interest in energy conservation devices. These devices range from fuel-efficient motors that use less oil, gas, and electricity, to controls that adjust use to meet specific environmental factors, such as mechanisms that turn on the heat in the morning and cut it down at night. Another example of how environmental forces can cause product innovation is the reduction of car size due to the desire to decrease energy consumption. This ultimately made the mid-sized car more desirable. Safety is yet another environmental factor that has led to the introduction of new features and innovations. Today many products have controls that prevent people from injuring themselves.

The list goes on and on, but the message is clear: Product innovation is an excellent means of extending market life and of preventing the attractiveness of a market from deteriorating too rapidly. Product innovation can be a winning strategy, but there are certain conditions that must be met:

— The new product must add to overall increased demand and not just to a redistribution of demand. This is particularly true of the leader, who won't gain if, by increasing demand on the new product, he reduces demand for the existing one (unless the demand for the existing product is in serious decline already). This was illustrated in Chapter 4 when I discussed the dilemma of Gillette in competing against Bic: Gillette could have introduced the throwaway razor and merely substituted sales of its traditional blades for the fully disposable unit introduced by Bic. This shows that the leader must be able to plot where he is on the life cycle, and not introduce the innovation too soon.

— The feature must be protectable and not easily imitated; or, if it is followed, it must demand investment and commitment from your competitors. Again, you are interested in sustained growth, not merely a temporary slip in demand. Furthermore, the innovation must enable the leader to protect his position. If it offers no protection, then the investment may be wasted.

SITUATION II: INNOVATION TO DISCOURAGE THE COMPETITION

In addition to breathing new life into a market, product innovation can be used to defend position by forcing the competition to invest heavily just to stay even, thereby increasing the cost of entry and of continued participation. This strategy is particularly effective in capital-intensive markets or where innovation is expensive and takes time to implement. Assume that you are the market leader in business data processing systems, or in sophisticated office equipment. You recognize that the product needs to be improved, and you have strong evidence that one of your major competitors plans to introduce a new feature that will make the equipment easier to use. You estimate that the competitor will have his new version within 18 months and that when it is introduced it will cut into your sales. Your strategy is to apply sufficient resources to get your own improved version ready within a 12- to 15-month period—not to introduce it prematurely but to bring it out at a critical time that will enable you to retain your leadership image, hold market share, and discourage your competition. Timing is crucial, so you don't want to be too early or too late. Some companies even wait until the competition puts its product on the market and then follow immediately with their own. This is based on the premise that the customer would prefer the identical features from the leader rather than from the unknown follower. The critical success factors are market and customer *intelligence* and *rapid response*—plus a willingness to continue to invest to maintain your leadership.

There is significant evidence that IBM uses this type of "stake raising" product innovation. IBM appears to invest in product improvements only to put them on the shelf until they are needed. There have been a number of times when the "seven dwarfs" (the nickname for its seven competitors—Sperry Rand, Honeywell, National Cash Register, RCA, GE, Control Data, and Burroughs) introduced a new feature, only to be rapidly followed by IBM. Thus, just when competitors thought that they were going to take share, IBM outbid them and prevented them from capitalizing on their innovations. This has always forced the competition to play catch-up ball by constantly raising the stakes, and ultimately the seven dwarfs were reduced to five. Obviously IBM was able to "quick follow" any innovation by its competitors because it was always ready with a similar innovation of its own.

Polaroid seems to have used the same strategy against Kodak. Although Kodak was larger and financially stronger than Polaroid, it refused to follow Polaroid into the instant camera market for a number of reasons. But everyone knew that as soon as the instant camera market grew, Kodak would enter it. But Kodak wanted to develop its own version, not to introduce the peel-off, time-exposure film camera that Polaroid already had on the market. Further, since Kodak produced the Polaroid film, it was already a profitable business. However, Polaroid didn't wait for its model to be made obsolete, and it began work on a new version of the camera, now known as the SX-70. The SX-70 series was introduced months before Kodak introduced its new model and, as a result, Kodak found that its new version was overpriced and obsolete as soon as it was introduced.

At the same time, Polaroid moved into a traditional Kodak stronghold—the movie camera market—thereby forcing Kodak to fight a "two-front" war. Polaroid attacked the movie market with an entirely new, revolutionary design. It timed its counterattack and aggressive growth in a way that would cause multiple problems for Kodak.

Situation III: Leapfrogging—Changing the Rules of Competition

Figure 6–3 depicts the purpose of an innovative "leapfrog" strategy. Suppose that you are in a poor position, or are not participating at all, in a market that seems to have a high sales and profit potential. Suppose that the market leader is strong and holds an impregnable position because of product, production, or marketing, and that he can't be assailed by a price-oriented strategy, because he has a cost position that permits him to price low and still make a profit. Suppose that he has traditionally refused to use umbrella pricing.

In this kind of situation, a viable strategy may be to seek out and develop a different approach to the product and process. This innovative approach must bypass the current leader's patents and force him to follow you. It must meet the

Figure 6-3. Diagram of a "leapfrog" strategy, moving from a weak to a strong position through innovation.

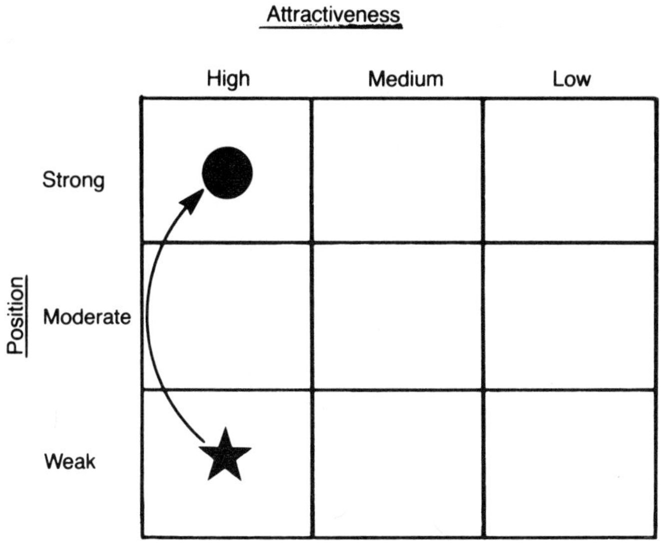

customer's expectations and needs so well that distributors and dealers will be willing to carry your line, even if they antagonize the current leader by doing so. Furthermore, the new product must enable you to force the current leader to increase rather than decrease costs. Let's examine some successful illustrations of companies that used technology to unseat the market leaders.

Locomotives. In the early years of the railroads, steam was the only source of power to drive locomotives. Naturally, the steam locomotive monopolized the market, and the leaders were Baldwin and American Locomotive. No manufacturer of steam-driven locomotives could hope to displace these two giants, but when General Motors designed and introduced the diesel locomotive, it changed the rules of the game by applying a more advanced technology. Today, GM has over 75% of the market, and Baldwin locomotives are in the Smithsonian Institution. Thus, the new technology resulted in a new leader.

Office Machines. In the 1950s, Kodak and Addresso-graph-Multigraph dominated the office copying business by using a wet, difficult-to-use, and poor-quality process. Then, Xerography was introduced by a little-known small company called Haloid, whose success is now a recorded fact. At the same time, Smith Corona, Underwood, Remington, and Royal were the leaders in manual office typewriters. IBM had never made a manual typewriter. Today IBM is the leader in the office typewriter market, having used an electric-power typewriter to displace the leaders. As a result, the original leaders have all been absorbed by other companies, and some have stopped producing office typewriters altogether.

Radios. When radios used tubes and were powered by house electricity, RCA Victor, Admiral, Philco, and Motorola were the market leaders. With the introduction of transis-torized, battery-powered radios, Japanese companies like Panasonic and Sony penetrated the market and took over the leadership position. Today, none of the previous leaders manufactures radios.

Aircraft. Piston-driven engines were the domain of Curtiss-Wright and Ford. But the introduction of the jet engine has resulted in the engine field's being shared by General Electric, Pratt & Whitney, and Rolls Royce.

The message here is clear: Leaders can be displaced by product innovation. But there are a number of similar situations in which success was not achieved, often as a result of poor timing.

Automobile Engines. The internal combustion engine has dominated the automobile since the early 1900s, having displaced the steam- and electric-driven cars. In the late 1960s, Mazda introduced its Wankel-type rotary engine, which was initially accepted by consumers because it was quieter and less of a pollutant, although it used more gasoline. Mazda was so successful that GM and Ford initiated their own development programs. Then came the energy crisis, which gave the rotary engine a serious blow, because consumers were more concerned with gas conservation than with noise and air pollution. Today, Mazda is just another imported, traditionally powered small car, though it still has hope of introducing the rotary engine in a new prestige line of cars.

Nuclear Power. Although the conventional nuclear power reactor has hardly been a smashing commercial success, the gas-cooled nuclear reactor has been even less successful. About ten years ago, General Atomics introduced the gas-cooled reactor as a substitute for the boiling-water–cooled reactor. Despite billions of dollars of investments and a subsequent merger with Gulf and Shell, General Atomics has never been able to gain a significant share of the market.

Building Products. Recognizing the escalating cost and time delays of building conventional "stick-built" houses, many companies have attempted to construct modular homes in factories and to ship them to site. It was believed that this new construction approach would be cheaper, faster, and an improvement—but it has never been a successful substitute because of local zoning laws and labor union resistance.

In summary, to be successful in leapfrogging and displacing the market leader, you must have:

— A truly unique, protectable product which meets customers' expectations and could entice them to switch.
— A competitor who is complacent, distracted, or dedicated to his current technology. This complacency or distraction may be a result of other corporate problems or of the fact that this business is the corporation's "cash cow" (a business that is expected to provide more than its fair share of cash). As a result of this complacency, the competitor may allow you to penetrate the market with a substitute technology or a new product.
— A risk-oriented management that recognizes that the leapfrog may fail.
— A willingness to invest for the period required, which may demand considerable cash flow and years of profitless growth.
— A dedicated, knowledgeable management. In a large corporation, this requires a sponsor with corporate clout.

— Applications and service to assure that the customer becomes your best salesman. This means that you must educate him and his staff and thereby make him a successful user.

SITUATION IV: DEVELOPING A NEW MARKET

In creating an entirely new market, the objective is to add to the total growth of the market, not to cause the growth of one product at the expense of another. For decades Du Pont has had a strategy of creating new products and creating new markets. Through its chemical expertise, Du Pont has been able to develop fabrics and textiles that have provided new functions and have gone way beyond merely being substitutes for the natural fibers. Nylon, rayon, and Corfam were all man-made fibers that have substituted for natural materials, but they added to market growth. Thus, Du Pont created new markets and, with the advent of new competitors, entirely new industries. Du Pont created an attractive new market and simultaneously became the segment leader. (See Figure 6–4.)

Color television was an RCA innovation that created an entirely new product line. Although it was initially a substitute for monochrome sets, today color has become the primary outlet for family viewing, and black and white has become the second set. RCA had all the pieces required to create the color market: the programming expertise to create programs; the technical ability to develop the required cameras, consoles, and monitors; the network, NBC, to broadcast the programs using the equipment it had developed; and the willingness to create user demand to acquire color television receivers.

In the mid-1970s, Sony introduced a direct video recording tape system, which permitted consumers to record their favorite programs directly from the television receivers. This was a brand new market that was not served by any other instruments. Sony's system, called Betamax, has prompted many other companies to follow suit and offer comparable sets, and has caused all the TV receiver manufacturers to purchase sets and market them under their own names.

Figure 6-4. Developing a new market.

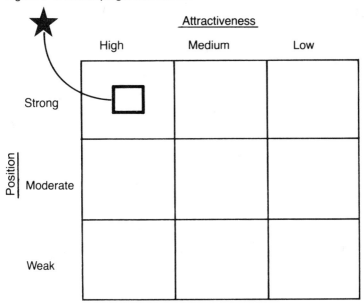

Zenith, for instance, has sourced products from Sony, RCA from Matsushita. In addition, RCA has delayed the market introduction of its video disc recorder, despite the fact that it had invested millions of dollars in developing the system.

Of course, the best illustrations of inventions that created entirely new markets were those of the early 1900s. Edison's incandescent lamp created a multibillion-dollar electrical industry. Similarly, Bell's invention created the telephone industry, and Ford's launched the automobile industry. This process continues to this day as companies are attempting to create an entirely new information and personal computation industry, which will most likely grow and become another multibillion-dollar industry. It remains to be seen whether this industry will be dominated by its founder or by a latecomer. At the early stages of market development there are usually many small entrepreneurs, each committed to its own special approach. But these can't all be successful and ultimately one or two versions will win out. Unfortunately, the original inventors may never reap the rewards of their innovations.

SITUATION V: LICENSING AIMED AT ESTABLISHING
A NEW INDUSTRY STANDARD

Many businesses make a significant part of their profit selling accessories, related services, or repair and spare parts. Profits are usually highest for the market leader and/or innovator. In this case the strategy emphasizes innovation, followed by extensive licensing aimed at making the product the industry standard. When the product standard has been established, the innovating company develops the market not only to sell its own finished products but also to sell accessories, services, spare parts, and key components. Again, Eastman Kodak is a good example. Kodak has innovated many cameras aimed at the novice photographer and mass market. These cameras are designed for ease of operation and are priced in the low to medium range. After introducing a camera and establishing a reputation as innovator, Kodak moves rapidly to license all the camera manufacturers, thereby obtaining revenues to pay back the investment made to develop the camera. At the same time, in so doing, Kodak ensures a larger market for film, film-processing supplies, and even film-processing equipment. Kodak has been able to maintain its leadership position in all these areas, and has made high profits on them.

A decade ago Philips of Holland attempted to duplicate the Kodak approach in the audiocassette tape and equipment market. Philips had developed a certain size of tape and wished to have the industry use it, so it offered the licenses to anyone free of charge. Unfortunately, it didn't have the strengths or position of Kodak and, unable to compete against Japanese competition, was forced to withdraw from the tape manufacturing market.

Similar strategies, used in industrial, capital goods, and government markets, explain why companies strive to be first even if the venture is unprofitable in the short range.

SITUATION VI: RESPONDING TO LEGISLATION, REGULATION, AND ENVIRONMENTALLY CREATED OPPORTUNITIES

Product innovation isn't always the result of taking advantage of customer, market, or competitive actions and needs; an increasing number of innovations have been the direct result of governmental laws, regulations, and environmentally created opportunities.

For example, no consumer or automobile operator demanded a catalytic converter, but these devices were sold in the millions as a direct result of federal legislation that reduced the permitted level of emissions from automobiles. By the same token, municipalities didn't invest millions of dollars in improved sewerage systems because they wanted to, but because regulations forced them to reduce the amount of sewage they were dumping into the nation's waterways. Finally, power utilities didn't voluntarily reduce their sulfur emissions and add expensive filtering systems; they did so as a response to legislation.

Thus, new product innovation strategies have been made possible by increasing governmental interference, which has resulted in opportunities, not merely constraints and threats. Of course, governmental spending has also encouraged innovation: Some companies have grown solely on the development of new products for defense, aerospace, and social programs. The list of government-inspired innovations is impressive; it includes computers, electronics, new materials, microcircuitry, telemetry, optics, and lasers. Tax laws have spearheaded the development of innovative services, one of the most noteworthy of which is H & R Block, whose growth is a result of the problems that millions of taxpayers have in filling out their tax returns.

Options for Leadership

Being a product innovator does require certain talents. But these talents are a result of the leadership approach that you select, as well as your field of endeavor. One option is to invest in basic research and to develop a product from the initial concept to the final commodity. This is the strategy employed by large drug companies and chemical companies, such as Du Pont, but the same approach is used by Abbott Labs, Warner-Lambert, and G. D. Searle, all of which invest heavily in basic research in the hope of developing a proprietary drug or antibiotic.

This kind of development also requires skill in obtaining the Food and Drug Administration's approval. If such products are successful, they can be very profitable, since they will be prescribed heavily by physicians. Of course, this requires a talented, specialized, and informed sales force of "detail men" who will educate doctors on the value and the side effects of the drugs. Basic research takes time and can be very risky; it is only one of the ways to be an innovator.

A second option is to improve or to apply someone else's patents by means of either licensing or purchasing. Licensing can be very effective. Bausch & Lomb successfully converted the results of the Czechoslovakian Academy of Science's soft contact lens research into a multimillion-dollar, highly profitable business. American Optical is about to repeat this approach by using the patents of Union Corporation. We all know that Edison didn't invent the incandescent lamp, but that he was able to improve the product so that it became commercially viable. This shows that you don't need to be the pioneer to be the innovator.

A third option is to acquire the inventing company and add to its commercial viability. Or you may be willing to joint-develop a product and create a company that will be the innovator. Corning Glass and Owens-Illinois created Owens-Corning Fiberglas to develop and lead in the utilization of fiberglass technology. Today this jointly owned company is one of the innovative forces in fiberglass. In the early 1920s General Electric, Westinghouse, and Marconi pooled their patents to create the Radio Corporation of America, which was an innovator in radio and, later, in television.

A fourth option is to bring to a market a technology that was created for an entirely different purpose. The best illustration of this is the transistor, whose technology came from Bell Labs, but which has been applied by a number of other companies for purposes never imagined by the original inventors.

Each of these options has its own rewards and risks and demands particular skills. The do-it-yourself option requires knowledge of the scientific fundamentals, whereas licensing requires acceptance of someone else's ideas and concepts. This acceptance is difficult for many companies, and as a result they never follow through on the project. However, all these options require financial and legal strength to see the project to its completion and to protect it legally.

"Quick Follow" Strategies

Leading isn't the most effective strategy in all situations; at times, it is more effective to be a second entry but to be aggressive enough to wind up as the ultimate winner. Let's examine some situations that permit one to be a successful quick follower.

As I mentioned earlier, the inventor or innovator isn't always the winner: The leader may be too early or may not have the ability to make it in the long run. We all know that an innovative product takes time to be accepted as a substitute or even as an entirely new product. The customer must be educated and must be willing to risk using the product. Furthermore, the initial products may have a number of problems that need to be solved before the product is accepted. If the innovator can't solve these problems, his or her reputation may be irreparably damaged, and the customers may be so dissatisfied that they will never buy from that firm again.

In addition, the innovator may not have the financial and sales ability to develop the entire market, which could permit another company to wait in the wings until the market is developed before it decides to enter. But when it does decide that the time is right, it should enter aggressively and promptly take over leadership. There are a number of examples of this strategy. IBM appears to have permitted smaller companies to develop the small- and micro-computer market, and now IBM is moving in to grab hold of the leadership of that market. In the solar energy field, many innovators are concerned that the large energy companies are following this precise strategy. In automobiles, General Motors and Ford have permitted other companies to develop the small car segment, and those two giants are now ready to take over. As these examples show, the timing of "quick follow" may vary. It may be years before the leader decides to follow, but the strategy is still quick if it is early enough to unseat the front runner. "Quick follow" is thus relative, not absolute.

Another reason to "quick follow" rather than to lead is that there is uncertainty as to which technology may be the ultimate winner. In technically based markets, there are initially two or more competing technologies, which are sponsored by different companies, each seeking to have its own approach accepted as the industry standard. But rather than gamble, it makes more sense to let the two or three innovators fight it out, and then to pick the winner at the most propitious time. This may require you to carefully monitor all developments and then, at the right time, license or duplicate the winning technology.

There are a number of illustrations of this principle. In the video disc market, the Sony video player seems to have outmaneuvered that of Philips. Since it would have been expensive for Zenith to compete with RCA, MCA/Philips, and Sony, it waited and has now agreed to market Sony's equipment, a boon for both Zenith and Sony. In the nuclear industry, there are two competing nuclear reactor technologies, one developed by Westinghouse and the other by General Electric. Both Combustion Engineering and Babcock & Wilcox have licensed the Westinghouse design. I described earlier how Mazda attempted to revolutionize the automobile industry by using rotary engines. Both GM and Ford were positioning themselves to follow Mazda if they saw that there was consumer demand for this kind of automotive power.

The same kind of situation is occurring as a result of legislation and regulations. Thus, many companies are adopting a wait-and-see strategy reinforced by a readiness to respond quickly. Today, companies are being told to conform with laws that dictate the amount and type of energy they can use and that impose limitations on their workforce, safety, equipment, and environmental conditions. There is so much confusion about what can and can't be done that companies are waiting to see what happens. Since the results can mean the difference between survival and extinction, the companies are monitoring the situation and are prepared to conform when necessary.

Many companies have such a strong market position that customers will wait until the supplier provides the new product they want. This is normally reinforced by a concern about the long-term viability of the newcomer. If the customer must be assured of continuing supply, spare parts, or service, the market leader is in a position to follow rather than lead.

"Quick follow" strategies are risky, and are often tougher or more expensive to carry out than leadership strategies. First of all, you permit someone else to establish a beachhead that you may not be able to overcome. Second, the customer may prefer the innovator's product to the follower's, or the follower may not achieve the competitor's level of competence. Third, the "quick follow" strategy requires an ongoing monitoring system that has enough objectivity to be able to recognize that someone else is offering something new and valuable. This requires a carefully conceived trigger to initiate the action that is to follow. If timing is against you, you must be able to license the product or to get it somewhere else. But suppose that the innovator won't license or source the product; then the follower must either forgo the opportunity or copy the product, with the risk of being sued, which may create a poor image. Thus, there is a reward/risk trade-off that must be carefully evaluated.

"Slow or No Follow" Strategies

Yet another option is to refuse to follow, or to follow at your own pace. For many companies this option seems inconceivable, and it is rare for the technical staff to recommend this option. But there are a number of reasons why it makes sense to follow a "slow or no follow" strategy.

First, the market or business may be a low priority to your company. The concept of portfolio management means that a company has decided not to be "all things to all people" or to pursue all opportunities. Just because an opportunity is attractive doesn't mean that it is the *most* attractive one, or the necessary resources may be so difficult to obtain that it is impossible or impractical to pursue. Thus, rather than being an also-ran or a low-share competitor, a company may be wiser to resist participating at all.

Second, the market may have significant growth, but the nature of the competition may be unattractive. Suppose that there are already too many companies participating or planning to compete. This may result in aggressive pricing, excess capacity, and low profitability. Thus, it may be better not to follow at all. In addition, the prime competitor may already dominate or be in a position to dominate.

Third, a competitor may not have the resources to be successful; thus, it may be better to resist following. Of course it must be recognized that this assessment is based on the innovator's developing the market on his own, without the help of an outsider. We all know that the innovating company could be acquired or merged with a stronger company that may be positioned to develop the market. Or the small company may develop the market on its own and fail, only to be taken over by a large company, which would then take the leadership.

Fourth, customers are often reluctant to switch to a new, untried product because of their concern about its performance and the losses they will incur. Switching may also force a customer to replace existing equipment that still has significant life or utility. This is one of the major reasons that many manufacturers have refused to acquire more efficient and flexible computerized or computer-assisted machine tools: It would force them to exchange equipment that still runs, has already been depreciated, and costs little for equipment that would force them to assume debt and may disrupt their workforce and operations.

Fifth, just because there is an innovative product doesn't

mean that the total market will grow rapidly enough to justify participation. This may mean that one product will substitute for another and that overall growth may not occur.

The final reason for not following is that it really won't add to your strength or overall position. Some companies are so strong in marketing or manufacturing that innovation may be a distraction to them. The innovative thrust may confuse an organization and force it to decrease its other strengths. If you are already leading with a marketing-driven strategy, then you may wish to continue this thrust and use it to negate the new innovation indirectly.

But adopting a "no follow" or "slow follow" approach requires you to be objective and have a well-thought-out contingency plan. You should always ask yourself, "What if I am wrong?"; "What if the competitor does have the resources to pull it off?"; "What if the customer finds the economics of switching favorable?"; or "What if your marketing expertise is no match for the innovation?" If after making this assessment you find your own strategy lacking, then there are several options that you can pursue:

1. You may decrease price, increase promotion, or provide incentives to distribution to make your product more attractive, while you accelerate your efforts to follow.

2. You may strive to go one step further and develop an improved version of the innovator's product, while in the interim pricing aggressively and letting your customers know that it will be worth their while to wait.

3. You may admit that you made a mistake and then seek a license or a joint venture, or even try to acquire the innovator. This takes guts, but sometimes it may be the only way to recoup your losses.

In each case you must be decisive and keep track of what is going on. If you must change your strategy, do it with conviction and be realistic—it is the only way.

Table 6–1 provides a summary of all the most important points made in this chapter about innovation-based strategies.

Table 6–1.

Type	Situation
Innovative leadership	Preventing market segment or product from maturing too soon Discouraging the competition Leapfrogging—Changing rules Developing a new market or an entirely new business Responding to legislation and regulation Standardization
"Quick Follow"	Competitor isn't strong enough to win Several competing technologies Uncertainty over legislation
"Slow Follow" or "No Follow"	Low corporate or business priority Unattractive competitive climate Competitor is expected to fail Customer can't afford to switch or won't for a long period of time Declining market or insufficient increased growth Other strengths to drive strategy

Summary of innovation-based strategies.

Relative Position	*Critical Success Factors*
Leader or strong position Leader—Strong financially	Strong intelligence system Rapid response Willingness to continue to invest
Weak now, but has unique qualities necessary to become long-term winner	Unique, protectable product Complacent market leader Risk-oriented management Willing to invest for period required Dedicated, knowledgeable management Service
Leader in new product	Uniqueness Sustaining power
Leader or close second	Ability to capitalize in timely manner
Leader	Ability to license and make designs that conform to industry standard so accessories, spare parts, and services can be sold
Probably number one—and is able to respond quickly	Recognition of risk Ongoing monitoring system Contingency options
Moderate to low position	Monitoring and establishing sound contingency plans

7

Using Financing and Executive Talents

ALTHOUGH growth, defense, and harvesting strategies can be achieved by creativity in product, production, or marketing, there are many examples where success was a result of a company's financial and managerial creativity. In this chapter, I would like to describe situations in which these factors were the key ingredients.

Financially Driven Strategies

Changing the financial conditions of doing business can help you acquire or hold share and position. Suppose that you have a new product and that the customer is unwilling to risk his capital or cash on this unproven product. In this case you may wish to offer the product on a low-risk basis, such as leasing, which permits customers to try out the product without committing themselves to its long-term use and without tying up their own cash and capital.

Leasing Arrangements

This will be effective in any capital- or cash-intensive situation or where the products change often. For example, a company may need to invest in new machine tools or computers, or automated equipment, all of which are expensive and require capital. In this case, a "cash rich" equipment manufacturer may decide to lease rather than to sell outright. Normally, he will establish a subsidiary leasing company to provide the capital, and permit him to maintain a favorable debt-to-equity ratio. This leasing company retains title to the equipment or machinery and charges a rental fee to the user, who in turn doesn't need to use his own capital or cash. Further, he can expense rather than capitalize the cost. These expenses have tax advantages.

This strategic thrust creates a barrier and increases the cost of entering and participating in the market. It has been effectively demonstrated by IBM and Xerox. Both of these companies made leasing an industry standard for their markets at an early stage, and thereby effectively raised the cost of participating in copying and computing.

Various Leasing Options

There are a number of leasing options, each with its own advantages and disadvantages.

Straight leasing is like renting: The lessee merely uses the equipment and pays for the usage. The rates are normally high, and there are no commitments. When the lessee has finished with the equipment, the lessor removes it and installs it elsewhere. In most cases, there is a minimum period and a penalty charge if that period isn't completed.

Another variation is *leasing with an option to buy.* In this situation, the lessee builds up equity in the equipment and, if he decides to acquire, part of the leasing fee is credited toward the purchase. This encourages acquisition and reduces the risk to the lessor. In a way this option is similar to purchasing on credit.

CRITICAL RESOURCES FOR LEASING

Leasing requires several critical resources. First, if you are going to provide leasing, it is crucial that you have a financial position that is strong enough to sustain the thrust. Wiltex is an example of a company that was unable to do this. Wiltex—a tiny Norwalk, Connecticut company—provided a computer-controlled terminal for communications systems. It was reported to have a superior product and was able to lease its equipment to over 60 major U.S. corporations. But it became cash-short due to losses suffered in developing its second-generation equipment. In the first six months of 1977, it lost $2.5 million on sales of $3.9 million and was ultimately forced to seek financial assistance—and even to consider outright sale—in order to avoid bankruptcy.

Second, you need to have an accurate assessment of the match between your product and the customer's needs and expectations. You must constantly remember that you are the owner of the equipment and that if a number of customers discontinue their use of the equipment and return it to you, then you will be stuck. This means that you must keep your customers happy with the equipment and its results. The key to this is quality equipment and service to support usage, quick repairs, and spare parts. You may also have to provide education and on-location servicing technicians.

You must also have strong legal and contracting support. The contracts must be foolproof and must protect you from unreasonable cancellations, unusual and profitless service, or contractual requirements to provide backup or warranties.

Finally, you should have contingency plans and potential lessees lined up in advance. It may be crucial to have customers in line waiting for the equipment. Timing could mean the difference between success and failure.

MOVING FROM LEASING TO DIRECT PURCHASE

As I said, leasing is most appealing during the early life of a product or service with customers who have financial limitations. But when a product matures, direct purchase may be more attractive, particularly for financially strong customers.

This was illustrated in both the computer and the copier markets. When computers matured, customers were more knowledgeable and desired to acquire them. At first IBM refused to sell, but the federal government put pressure on it, not only as a regulator but also as a customer. The federal government was and is the largest user of computers. IBM finally agreed, and purchasing became an option. This has become the standard in the small and medium-size computer field. The same thing has occurred in the copier market: more and more companies have elected to purchase rather than to lease. This change has profoundly affected the capital and cash requirements of doing business, and has permitted smaller companies to compete effectively.

Offering Favorable Terms and Conditions of Purchase

Rather than expand a market or increase or maintain their share by pricing, many companies elect to use attractive terms and conditions of purchase. There are several options: They can provide favorable timing, attractive interest rates, or additional services, or they can accept products rather than cash.

TERMS OF PAYMENT: TIME PERIODS

Terms of payment can have strategic implications. A number of retail stores still require cash on delivery. In some cases cash means currency, whereas in others it may include credit cards. Some retailers, like Sears, emphasize and encourage credit—Sears's own credit cards are used in 54% of their purchases. This has strategic implications, since it influences the kind of customers you will serve and the amount of timing of their purchases, as well as the cash requirements of doing business.

Many companies that serve industrial, governmental, and commercial customers (and some that serve individual customers) demand "progress payments"—that is, payment before delivery. This is particularly true in capital-intensive, long-cycle businesses. For example, a company acquiring a large customized machine tool may pay before the work begins and again halfway along the manufacturing cycle. It must then pay *in full* before delivery is made. This strategy minimizes the risk and capital needs of the manufacturer, but it also restricts sales only to those who are able and willing to pay.

Other companies provide normal terms, like making payment 30 days after delivery. In some situations, the timing is 90 to 120 days. Obviously, the longer the time period, the more costly it will be to do business. There are even cases in which the manufacturer doesn't require payment until the goods are sold—this is called consignment. In simple terms, it means that the manufacturer holds title until the goods are sold and, in effect, stores the product in the customer's shop. When the customer (the retailer) sells the merchandise, the manufacturer pays the supplier. This is attractive for the retailer, since there is no risk and little cost.

TERMS OF PAYMENT: INTEREST

International and capital-intensive businesses are strongly influenced by the rate of interest. In the early days of the Marshall Plan and the Agency for International Development (AID), U.S. manufacturers had a strong competitive advantage because of financing rates. They were granted many loans with interest below commercial rates, or with no interest at all. These loans ran for decades, and some were forgiven outright. In today's international market other nations often offer more attractive interest rates than does the United States.

Obviously the rate of interest charged also affects the consumer and domestic commercial markets. Some companies charge nominal rates, whereas others charge top dollar. Some want to earn income on financing, and others want to use financing to support sales. Many companies have established subsidiaries to handle the financing aspects of their businesses. These subsidiaries have simultaneously aimed at increasing sales, establishing a competitive barrier, and generating a healthy additional income. Sears, for instance, has a highly profitable credit organization, as do General Motors and Ford. These credit organizations help finance purchases of the company's products at competitive rates. In some markets, the financial terms are the most important factor in making the sale. For example, in an effort to sell the Air Bus to U.S. airlines, the Air Bus Corporation is offering planes for an extended period at no cost. In return, the company expects the airlines' use of the Air Bus to increase awareness of the product.

TERMS OF PAYMENT: BARTER AND LOCAL MANUFACTURE

To sell to developing and Eastern European nations, you must either barter or enable the host nation to manufacture your product locally. These countries need products, but they are also interested in balancing their trade and income accounts and to increase their employment and self-sufficiency.

It may seem strange to many Americans that, as we enter the era of electronic funds transfers and of the "cashless society," barter is also increasing. Many countries are cash- and capital-poor, so they demand that part of the payment for consumer goods and for industrial equipment be in the form of goods or commodities. Japanese companies recognized this a long time ago and established trading companies, which are really giant export and import arms of Japan. They sell sophisticated drive systems, generating plants, computers, and electronics, and accept payment in foodstuffs, minerals, textiles, and so on. The manufacturer can be paid in yen or dollars, and the trading companies serve as intermediaries. In several Western European countries this function is performed by the government. Thus both Japanese and Western European manufacturers have created a strategic advantage over their American competitors: In most cases, American companies aren't capable of handling bartered goods.

Barter requires several specialized talents and, in order to be effective, it must be planned carefully. First of all, you must understand how to estimate the value of the bartered product. Most often the products aren't sophisticated, they are highly price-sensitive, and their value can fluctuate dramatically. It is like playing the commodity markets—you can either win or lose big. Second, the market for these products is normally outside the experience of the company that is selling the sophisticated technical product—its sales force just isn't capable of selling Polish hams, or wheat, or copper. Third, there are usually significant logistic problems in shipping the bartered goods, including complicated export/import licensing and other requirements.

TERMS OF PAYMENT: LOCAL MANUFACTURE

Even if customers will pay cash, they may demand that part of the product be made locally. Even though the customer will most often make the less complicated part of the product, there are several problems here. First of all, you must line up a local vendor who can be trained to manufacture the product to your specifications, and in sufficient quantity for your needs. Second, you must be sure that the local manufacturer doesn't become a major competitor, and this is often difficult to do. Third, you must make sure that you can legally take the products outside the country.

In some parts of the world, countries are demanding that an increasingly larger portion of the product be made locally. In Brazil, 90–95% local manufacture is demanded, but there are several possible ways to comply with this law. First, you can select and license a local company—this is similar to using a vendor in the United States. Second, you can establish a jointly owned company composed of local individuals or even of the government. This must be more than 50% locally owned, but it can be managed by you. Third, you might establish a wholly or majority-owned subsidiary as an initial entry and later increase local ownership or transfer ownership to the host government.

Equity Ownership

Earlier in this book I discussed the advantages of having your own company-owned distribution, and I just reviewed how ownership may be critical in certain foreign countries. Owning either your customers or those who are between you and your product users isn't new: In the early stages of any industry, it is common to find the customer partially or completely owned by the supplier or manufacturer. Both Edison and Bell used equity as a means of going into a market and permitting the distributor to acquire capital-intensive and expensive equipment. Utilities aren't normally considered distributors, but they are, and often perform the distributor's function: They generate power in bulk and break it down into small pieces for their users.

The Edison General Electric Company was an equity owner of its customers. In fact, all those utilities with the Edison name were partially or wholly owned by Edison GE, and the customers received equity in return for their stock. This ownership strategy was followed until 1893, at which time the stock was transferred to the Electric Bond & Share Corporation. Edison had learned that this was the way to finance the growth of the market. Bell Telephone used a similar approach, and has continued it to this day. AT&T owns a large number of local telephone companies and has direct contact with its users, whereas General Electric—the successor to Edison GE—does not.

Financially Driven Strategies: Conclusions

In conclusion, financially driven strategies can be extremely effective means of making a market grow, increasing share, and creating a competitive barrier. The key is money and access to money at competitive rates for a sufficient period of time. (The period of time is sufficient if it effectively discourages the competition and if the product then becomes the industry standard.) The use of your financial strength must be suited to the market needs. If you give too much credit, or accept the risk of barter or ownership too easily, you will detract from your own profitability.

These same techniques can be used to hold or defend position as well. As with innovation or low-cost strategies, you can wait until the competitor thinks he has success within reach—and then raise the stakes. This reluctant but "quick follow" approach can work just like a new product improvement. Timing is critical, along with the monitoring of customer need and competitors' actions.

If you wish to gradually harvest, then financial terms, conditions, and interest can be gradually escalated. If you are the leader, expect your competition to follow. This could limit market growth and permit you to hold share or, if the raise is more abrupt, you may use this approach to increase cash and earnings.

Executive-Driven Strategies

The final kind of driver that I will discuss is based on executive talent and leadership. Just as in football or basketball, strategic moves can be the result of the skill of the coach. When to merge, acquire, enter a joint venture, or divest is a critical executive decision that can be the driving force of a company, spelling the difference between success and failure.

Acquisitions and Mergers

An article in *Business Week* * described many of the reasons for the mergers and acquisitions of the 1970s. It differentiated this period from the conglomerate growth phase of the 1960s, pointing out that one of the major differences was that in the 1970s, the acquiring companies were more mature and more financially solvent. Let's examine some of the reasons for such a strategy of merger or acquisition.

Current business portfolios often have too many poorly positioned businesses and not enough long-growth sales and income generators. Furthermore, businesses have discovered that even today's "cash cows" will run dry in the future. As a result, many companies have decided to acquire firms that make relatively new products and that, if given enough funding, can be used to create the future sales and earnings growth desired.

Since 1951, Beatrice Foods has been following this kind of acquisition strategy. At that time, Beatrice was a cash-rich, slowly growing dairy products company that decided to diver-

* November 14, 1977.

sify rather than either invest in commodity businesses or move head on against Kellogg's or Campbell's. Beatrice has sought a variety of companies that have one major characteristic—they are profitable and well managed. Furthermore, it looks for companies that can be acquired relatively inexpensively and that can benefit from Beatrice's financial, managerial, and control strengths. It maintains the current management, keeps the current brand name, and doesn't link the product with Beatrice. Its acquisitions have included dairy and food companies, such as Hotel Bar butter, Louis Sherry ice cream, and Clark bars; leisure industry companies, like Morgan yachts, Airstream trailers, and Hart skis; and other manufacturing companies, like Samsonite luggage and Stiffel lamps. In 1976 Beatrice had sales of over $2.5 billion; it has increased its sales at a 13% per annum rate and its income at 15% per year over a 25-year period.

Another dairy company also changed its product mix by diversifying into other foods and chemicals. In 1974, a recession year, Borden made more than half of its earnings from chemicals. However, unlike Beatrice, Borden has tied all its products to its own name.

REDUCING OVERDEPENDENCE THROUGH DIVERSIFICATION

Profitability of industry specialists undoubtedly exceeds that of the diversified companies, both on the average and in "good" years. But specialists are highly vulnerable to cycles and can be deeply hurt by off-years. Furthermore, in the era of legislation and governmental control, such firms can be wiped out. This point can be illustrated by two events that took place in 1976–1977: One was the ban on Tris in children's sleepwear; the other was the ban on saccharine. Both of these actions did considerable damage, even throwing some specialists into receivership. Yet another reason for not becoming too specialized is your increased vulnerability to foreign dumping. This is the problem of Zenith and of American steel companies.

The answer, then, is to diversity—to move out of the specialist category and into the multi-industry class. For example, Studebaker lost the automobile race and, rather than collapse, it merged with Worthington. In recent years, this merged company has made several acquisitions, including Wagner Electric. Today, Studebaker-Worthington's portfolio includes Gravely Division, Compressor Division, Clarke Division, Pump Division, Onan Division, Masonelian Division, STP, Turbine Division, and Wagner.

In 1963, Kidde Corporation had sales of $40 million; in 1976, its sales had reached $1.2 billion. Kidde today has consumer and commercial products including Farberware, Progress Lighting, Spartus, Waltham, Rexair, Arnex, and Vanity Fair, which contribute a total of $368 million (30% of Kidde's sales); safety, security, and protection equipment, which contributes $445 million (36% of sales) under the brand names of Sargent, Skum, LeFebure, PrestoLock, and Globe Security Systems; and industrial equipment sales of $418 million (34% of sales) under such brands as Grove, Dura, Garden State, Weber Aircraft, Brock Press, and New Jersey Office Supply. Thus, Kidde has a balanced, less cyclical mix of businesses, all derived by acquisitions.

The two largest soft drink companies, Pepsi and Coca-Cola, have taken a number of steps to become less concentrated. Pepsi has acquired a sporting goods company, a van lines, and a snack foods firm; Coke has added Taylor wines, a food company, and a Syracuse television station.

Oil companies have chosen a variety of ways to reduce their own dependence on oil:

— Mobil has acquired a majority interest in Marcor, a company that had previously been formed by a merger of Montgomery Ward and Container Corporation of America.
— Standard Oil of California acquired a 20% interest in Amax; while Union Oil of California purchased MolyCorp, a producer of molybdenum and rare earth materials.
— Exxon acquired companies in uranium and solar power to expand its energy holdings, and has pur-

chased companies involved in such areas as scholastic testing, instrumentation for measuring air pollution, graphite shafts for golf clubs, and voice and micro-computers.

— Gulf and Shell acquired General Atomics.

REDUCING COMPETITIVE THREATS OR IMPROVING MARKET POSITION

Mergers and acquisitions also occur to prevent competition from taking share or to increase share to the level required for the company to remain viable. There is significant evidence that market share is a valuable asset and that without a critical level of share, a company won't succeed.

There are a number of recent illustrations of this principle. In the television receiver business, Philips acquired Magnavox, Matsushita purchased Quasar from Motorola, and Sanyo acquired Warwick to strengthen its American market position. In Canada three companies in the appliance market—Canadian General Electric, GSW, Ltd., and Canadian Westinghouse—merged to increase their market share. This permitted the new company to increase share to 37% and to counteract the threat of imports, which had risen from 14.4% of the market in 1967 to 26% in 1975. Other recent examples of this kind of acquisition took place in the oil industry, where Getty acquired Mission and Skelley Oil, and Marathon acquired Pan Ocean Oil.

These kinds of acquisitions and mergers make a lot of sense and are the quickest way to increase share. Of course, they require a great deal of study, skill, and negotiations. You must first be certain that the merged parties are complementary, not redundant. If both components demand acquiescence from their new partners, then there will be considerable conflict and probably a weaker rather than a stronger company. However, if the companies concentrate on different segments and represent different skills, then a more synergistic and stronger company will result. For example, if a company concentrating on small and minicomputers merged with one whose strength was in medium and large computers, the marriage is likely to work. This kind of merger took place in the early 1890s when Thompson-Houston was a proponent of AC electrical transmission and was a leader in power traction—that is, electrical components for streetcars and elevated railways. Edison GE was strong in DC technology and was the leader in lighting. Together they created a stronger electrical company.

Obtaining governmental approval for the acquisition and merger is another important factor. The Justice Department is concerned about increasing concentration in any industry, and it may try to prevent any company from becoming too dominant. Depending on the administration and public opinion at the time, the chances of the government's allowing mergers to take place will vary. Some observers point out that even though the Democrats are thought to be tough antitrust enforcers and the Republicans are not, the opposite is true: There have been more antitrust actions and mergers fought when the Republicans are in power than when the Democrats are.

OPPORTUNISTIC MERGERS AND ACQUISITIONS

Sometimes a company is available for acquisition or merger and the deal is just too good to pass up. For instance, Nestle was seeking to expand its American product base, whereas Stouffer's was looking for cash to expand. When Stouffer's approached Nestle to borrow, Nestle made an offer, Stouffer accepted, and Nestle added hotels, restaurants, and prestige frozen foods to its product portfolio.

In return for acquisition of Hartford Insurance, ITT was required by the court to divest itself of its Avis subsidiary. Norton Simon took advantage of this court ruling and acquired Avis, thus permitting it to participate in the automobile rental market. Atari had been successful in developing the television game market—so successful, in fact, that it didn't have the manufacturing, managerial, and financial resources to capitalize on its opportunity. Warner Communications came to the rescue and simultaneously picked up a new business. Babcock & Wilcox was being aggressively pursued by United Technologies, but was reluctant to be acquired by that firm. Rather than succumb to the undesired takeover, B&W agreed to merge with J. Ray McDermott. And so the list grows: Acquisitions are being consummated on a planned and unplanned basis. Quite often a company wants to participate in a given market but can't afford to develop the business itself. Tenneco, for example, owned Walker Manufacturing, a large automotive supplier. Tenneco was interested in increasing its scope; and when Monroe Auto Equipment, a leader in shock absorbers, became available, Tenneco seized the opportunity and acquired Monroe.

INTEGRATION: BACKWARD AND FORWARD

Companies have many good reasons for integration, including the desire to cut costs, guarantee supply, or solidify their control over dealers or distributors. At times, integration may be neither planned nor even desired, but it may be required by circumstances. This is true when a supplier or distributor is on the verge of bankruptcy or being sold to a competitor. The only option may be acquisition.

Partnerships as Alternatives to Acquisitions

In discussing the need for local manufacture in foreign countries, I mentioned that partial ownership, joint ventures, and consortiums have become popular. There are opportunities that two equally strong companies may wish to pursue, but neither one may have the total resources necessary or the willingness to assume risks. Some opportunities require billions of dollars and are beyond the ability of even the industrial giants—this has been the case for many years in the petroleum development and exploration field. Explorations in the North Sea and Alaska have required the formation of consortiums of many oil companies and even the participation of national governments. Uranium mining has been undertaken by jointly owned electric utilities. Construction of cities and ports in Saudi Arabia and Kuwait has required the formation of consortiums representing construction companies, electric and telephone companies, and consulting engineering firms. In some parts of the world, this is the only way bids will be accepted, and if you wish to participate you must join a consortium or elect not to bid at all.

Jointly owned companies have also become popular. Allis-Chalmers has created several new companies with foreign partners. In farm equipment Allis has joined with Fiat, and in the power equipment field it has joined with Siemens. I mentioned earlier that Westinghouse joined with Tenneco to form the Offshore Power Corporation. MCA and Philips have formed a joint venture in the video disc business: MCA has the software and libraries, and Philips has the technology and equipment to manufacture the product.

Another illustration of joint ownership was Siemens's and Corning Glass's formation of Siecor Optical Cables to produce optical waveguide cables (a substitute for conventional copper cables) and related hardware for the communications industry. Amory Houghton, their president, stated: "We put in our technology and other people put in their downstream capabilities and marketing savvy—things we don't have." * Joint venturing makes sense to Corning Glass as a means of reducing risks and of enhancing success.

None of these approaches are really new: Joint ventures and consortiums have been used in military and space contracts for many years. But they are a strategic option and can be extremely powerful if they are properly selected and are matched with the appropriate implementation strategies.

What Does It Take to Succeed?

All these management strategies require specific talents. Acquisitions and mergers, as well as joint ventures, are similar to marriages: To be successful they require intelligent, consenting, and cooperative adults who know what they want, recognize their strengths and limitations, and are willing to compromise. Shotgun marriages rarely work, and neither do forced takeovers.

If an acquisition moves a company into a new, unknown

* *Forbes,* August 1, 1977.

market, it may be critical for the current management to be retained. If it is doubtful whether the current management will stay on after such a move, then a back-up management team should be chosen or the acquisition should be reevaluated—or even aborted.

Another critical decision focuses on how much the acquired or merged company will be integrated and to whom it will report: Will it retain its own identity? Will it keep its own policies and practices? Or will it be forced to comply with the practices of the acquiring company? Beatrice Foods, for example, has made it a rule to keep its acquisitions separate. Beatrice merely requires a clear set of objectives and goals. If the acquired company meets the goals, it is left alone; if it fails to meet these goals, it is given help, but is still considered separate. Every attempt is made to retain the management. This is difficult, but Beatrice has proved that it can be done. Other companies have the opposite approach: The acquired company loses its independent status, it is labeled a "division" or "subsidiary" of the parent company, and is subjected to the rules and regulations of the parent. In most cases the management leaves. This approach, too, can succeed, but it takes a toll on both parties. It may be disastrous if the acquired company isn't gradually integrated into the acquiring company. This requires that the new company be given guidance from a senior member of the new parent's management, that its information system be integrated, and that clear lines of delegation and responsibility be established. The acquired company can't remain a stepchild.

Since mergers and acquisitions have become so important and the dollar accounts involved so large, there has emerged a corps of specialists who identify targets and negotiate takeovers, or even help companies resist takeovers. These skills can be vital in large ventures, and can spell the difference between success and failure.

The Other Side: Dispositions and Pruning

Disposition and sale of a business is one of the divestiture and exit options available. It can be achieved in the form of pruning products, segments, or total businesses. Although to a layman it may appear simple, disposing of a business is an arduous, emotional task. Let's review some of the reasons a corporate executive may wish to exit from a business.

Some companies may wish to cut their losses and concentrate on their winning businesses. In fact, the cash generated by the sale may be channeled into more attractive and promising products. For example, San Francisco's Fibreboard Corporation sold its unprofitable folding carton division to reduce its losses and invest the cash generated by the sale into other businesses. The folding carton business was reported to have had losses of $6 million on sales of $263 million.* Its sale caused an extraordinary loss of $26 million in write-offs, but increased the cash reserves of the company by $30 million.

Similarly, Rohm & Haas sold its Fayetteville, N.C. synthetic fiber plant to Monsanto Company for $55 million to provide a financial boost to its specialty chemical business. † It also sold its modestly profitable Warren-Teed Pharmaceutical subsidiary for $16.5 million to generate additional cash. These moves will enable Rohm & Haas to concentrate on its chemical businesses—polymers, resins, plastics, herbicides, and pesticides.

Another reason to divest is to sell off businesses that don't fit the total corporate portfolio. This action is especially effective when the businesses are healthy and growing, since they can be sold at a premium. Only a decisive and strategically planned company can take such an action because it means exiting a real and potential winner. In a sense this is what ITT elected to do when it was willing to sell Avis and Levitt. Avis was profitable and strong.

At other times, a sale may be purely opportunistic—one company may want to own a business that you are in, and will pay you handsomely for it. The danger is that you may become greedy and mortgage the company's future for short-term profits.

But whatever the reason for disposition, you must always remember that even your losing businesses have value and, if fact, they may be more valuable to someone else. Thus, you

* *Business Week,* December 6, 1976.
† *Business Week,* October 31, 1977.

should determine the most profitable means of exiting. Let's consider some of the options available to you.

Option I: Outright Sale

This may be best accomplished by identifying those who are already in the business or who want to enter it. Westinghouse's appliance business was a major asset to White Consolidated (WCI), which was already in the business. Westinghouse had a good brand and a stronger dealer and service network than did WCI. Thus, Westinghouse's problem was an asset for WCI. I already mentioned the Quasar-Matsushita deal in which Quasar doubled Panasonic's share in the American market. IBM was required to sell its Service Bureau to another computer company, Control Data, thus enabling Control Data to expand its product and service offerings.

Option II: Spin-off with Declining Equity

At times the acquiring company may have inadequate financial resources or be concerned about the worth of the business. In this case, it may decide to spin off the business, creating a separate company and selling a share to the potential purchaser. The size of the equity sold may be tied to the ability of the purchaser to pay, as well as to the timing of the transition. This was the approach taken by General Electric in its disposition of its Computer Division to Honeywell. A new jointly owned company was formed—Honeywell Information Systems. GE owned 18% of the stock and agreed to liquidate its holdings in three years.

Thus, there is a gradual transition of ownership, the purchaser has more time to pay, and he can even use business profits to pay off the seller. This approach also gives the purchaser confidence that the business is healthy and that he isn't getting a lemon. In some instances, the original owner maintained his equity and ultimately took back ownership.

Option III: Sale to Employees

One of the major obstacles in any sale is the insecurity of the employees. Employees have the greatest stake in the business, and at times they are capable of turning a profitless business into a profitable one. Thus, it makes sense to offer the business to the employees for purchase. Here are examples of two companies that had decided to sell off some of their retail stores, and that sold a percentage of them to their employees. Goodrich decided to deemphasize its tire business and reinvest the cash in its chemical businesses. As part of this deemphasis, it decided to close down or sell its company-owned tire and appliance stores, which weren't meeting management's desired profitability levels. Many of the stores were eventually taken over by employees who switched from being professional managers to being entrepreneurs. Results have been profitable for both. A&P also decided to reduce its urban outlets, so it sold the stores to employees.

There are several other situations in which large corporations decided to exit a business because it was too small, was too unprofitable, or produced a product outside the corporation's desired portfolio. In each case, the employees took over and the businesses prospered. This option isn't reserved to retailing companies alone. Bell & Howell sold two of its subsidiaries—Bell & Howell Communications and Composite Microcircuits—to its management, while Sperry & Hutchinson sold its Interlock Furniture subsidiary to its president.

Conclusion

Both financial and executive options are available to drive a business toward successful growth, defending, harvesting, or exiting. As is the case in all other strategies, this one must be built on your own strength or on a competitor's deficiency. Normally "me too" strategies lead to "me too" results, and that isn't enough.

PART III

Functional Decisions and Total Strategy Integration

8

Implementation Strategies

SINCE it is the combination of an investment and management strategy that determines the appropriate implementation strategies, I would like to summarize the viable options which may be selected. It is obvious that all management strategies cannot be used with every investment strategy and that some of their characteristics will change with the investment strategy selected. In general, better management strategies are available for a growth/penetration strategy than for harvesting or exiting.

Investment/Management Strategy Combinations

Growth Strategy Options

Growth strategies are aimed at influencing market size, influencing the growth rate of the market, increasing share, or possibly all three. It is most appropriate at the early stage

Figure 8-1. When growth strategies fit the life cycle.

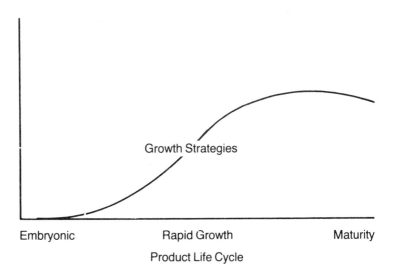

Embryonic   Rapid Growth   Maturity

Product Life Cycle

of the product life cycle, often called the embryonic stage, and in the rapid growth phase or even the maturity stage. (See Figure 8–1.)

MARKETING STRATEGIES

New want identification, which enables a company to capitalize on its market research and its ability to satisfy new demands, is an effective way to grow.

In *demand creation and influencing,* growth can be achieved by advertising, promotion, and training customers to use and apply the product in increasing frequencies or for an increasing range of uses.

Aggressive/learning-curve pricing stimulates growth by making the product or service affordable to a larger number of users.

Broad, expansive distribution aids product growth by increasing the availability of the product and ease of purchase.

Service-based strategies increase the customer's confidence and extend the amount of time he can use the product.

Geographic/segment expansion increases volume and often share by broadening the scope and number of customers who can buy.

Prestige pricing and limited, specialized distribution can be used to increase share in the prestige "niche," but are inappropriate to volume expansion strategies.

PRODUCTION-BASED STRATEGIES

Capacity in advance of demand can be a powerful way to increase share at the expense of those with limited or no capacity to capitalize on the demand, especially in capital-intensive, long-cycle businesses.

Process innovation can be used to increase share and, coupled with capacity expansion, can also contribute to market growth.

Readiness to serve can achieve the same results as capacity expansion, since it provides a way to take share from competitors who are unwilling to stock in advance of demand or to stock rapidly enough to meet demand.

Capacity utilization, manufacturing efficiency, and backward integration can all inhibit flexibility and aim at cost reduction at the expense of growth. These are inappropriate to growth.

PRODUCT-BASED STRATEGIES

Leadership in the form of "leapfrogging" or features evolution can create new demand or interest in the product as well as increase share. The degree of aggressiveness will vary. Thus product-based strategies will have differing risk and reward characteristics. It is also inappropriate to lead in standardization, which can enhance sales of accessories and related services.

"Quick follow" technology and product options can also be an effective way to increase share at the expense of weaker competitors who lack the ability to take advantage of their leadership.

"Slow-" or "no-follow" strategies are inappropriate alternatives.

Figure 8-2. When hold/defend strategies fit the life cycle.

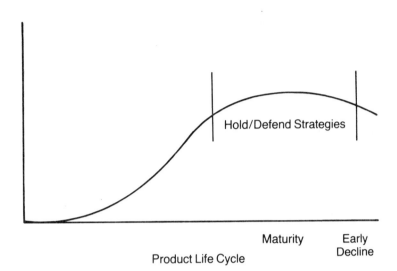

FINANCIAL/EXECUTIVE GROWTH OPTIONS

Favorable financial terms and conditions, leasing, and barter can produce the same results as lowering price, since they allow a large number of customers to afford the product. On the executive side, the use of acquisitions, mergers, and joint ventures aimed at expanding market or product coverage will all contribute to growth.

Hold/Defend Management Strategies

Holding and defending investment strategies are most appropriate for strong, profitable companies in the mature and early stages of declining product cycles. (See Figure 8–2.)

DEFENSIVE MARKETING STRATEGIES

Need/want identification can be used to defend a position by enabling the leader to be one step ahead of the competition. This requires anticipating and satisfying needs in a timely and responsive way.

Demand creation—selective, periodic use of advertising,

promotion, training, and applications enhancement—can also be an effective means of holding position.

Moderately aggressive pricing can raise the cost of competitors' aggressiveness, thus forcing a retrenchment.

Distribution strategies, aimed at maintaining a strong, loyal distribution/dealer network, have proved to be an effective defense against the opportunistic aggressor. This may require acquiring dealers to prevent them from switching to another brand.

Services can create a barrier that increases the cost of participating in the market. This may include rapid response or low-cost repair services. It is costly to maintain a network of services, facilities, and trained personnel.

Geographic/segment redefinition strategies trade off one segment or region for another. This will hold overall volume, though a company may actually gain share in one segment and give it up in another.

Prestige pricing and selective distribution are possible for a "niche" approach but are not effective across-the-board strategies.

PRODUCTION DEFENSE STRATEGIES

Capacity in advance and process innovation can be used to keep the cost of participating high and thus build a barrier to discourage new and existing competition.

Capacity utilization, manufacturing efficiency, supply assurance, deployment, and readiness optimization are all effective means of decreasing the cost of manufacturing and serving the customer and thereby reducing prices or increasing services or even promotion. Thus these strategies are supportive of another strategy rather than being prime drivers. However, in some situations mere recognition by the competition that a company has the lowest cost position often deters aggressiveness.

PRODUCT OPTIONS TO HOLD POSITION

Both selective, evolutionary innovation and "quick follow" strategies can enable a company to hold share. Standardization, another means of reducing costs, can have the same impact as the efficiency and utilization strategies described above.

Financial/executive strategies may permit a company to defend its position by acquiring product lines, distribution networks, and even competing or complementary companies. Of course, setting attractive payment terms or conditions or moving from leasing to outright purchase may suffice. The key is to do only enough to make the difference, not so much to reduce profits.

Harvest strategies are aimed at gradually giving up share or riding out a declining market. Thus this option is selected when market growth has stabilized and is declining slowly. (See Figure 8–3.) It may also be chosen when a weaker competitor recognizes that it is vulnerable and is permitted by the leader to sell off share over time.

Harvesting via Marketing Management Strategies

By gradually decreasing the amount spent on advertising, promotion, or distribution, or decreasing the number of ser-

Figure 8-3. When harvesting fits the life cycle.

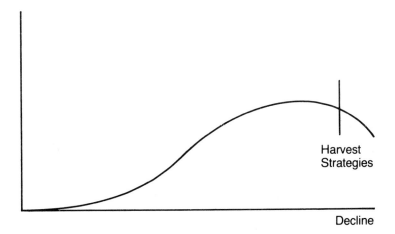

Harvest
Strategies

Decline

Product Life Cycle

vice and distribution centers, a company may be able to increase its net income by selling off its market position. Increasing prices or charging for services and warranties previously included in the initial selling price (referred to as unbundling) can have the same results. Thus demand creation, high pricing, distribution service, and geographic contraction all permit slow harvesting.

PRODUCTION-DRIVEN HARVESTING OPTIONS

Emphasizing high utilization and refusing to invest in new plant and equipment are effective means of harvesting the business. Manufacturing efficiency, supply assurance, and reduced inventories may selectively be used—provided that they do not increase investment and decrease profitability. If they are not selective, harvesting will change into a hold or even a growth strategy.

Capacity-in-advance and process-innovation strategies are the antithesis of harvesting.

PRODUCT-DRIVEN HARVESTING

Product leadership and "quick follow" strategies are normally inappropriate, since they are more expensive than the results justify. Sometimes a selective innovation may be required if the harvest is expected to span a number of years and the competition requires a response. This may be a "slow follow" or even a copy strategy. The "slow-" or even "no-follow" options are most appropriate in a supportive role to another driver.

FINANCIAL/EXECUTIVE-DRIVEN OPTIONS

The use of attractive or even competitive terms and conditions does not fit harvesting. Giving only what is required—and, if possible, less than the average—is the best fit. On the executive side, the disposition or pruning of segments and product lines can be the best way to give up over time. It is planned withdrawal from the battlefield.

Figure 8-4. When divest/exit strategies fit the life cycle.

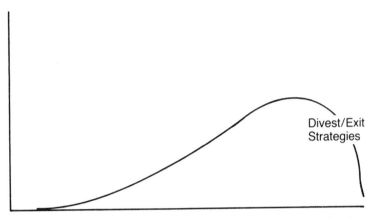

Divest/Exit
Strategies

Rapid Decline

Product Life Cycle

Divest/Exit Strategies

The divest or exit option may be executed at any stage of the life cycle by weak competitors, but is used only in the rapidly declining phase by the leader. (See Figure 8–4.)

There are much fewer options for this strategy than any other. Marketing strategies, in general, are not viable for exiting or divesting except to increase short-range share so as to make the business appear better to a potential buyer. At times it may make sense to exit the product manufacturing end of the business but to remain in the service or distribution side—for example, to serve the repair and replacement parts of a mature or declining market.

Production options are also limited. High and even excessive capacity utilization is the only reasonable solution. All other manufacturing alternatives are too expensive.

Product innovation is never an alternative. Engineering may not even exist in an exit business unless it is part of the

Figure 8-5. Implementation strategy: a conceptual view.

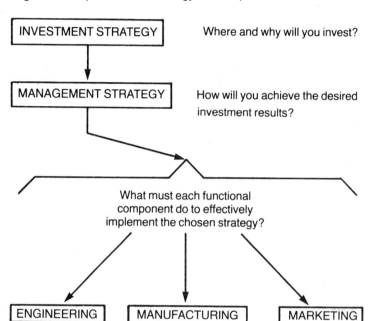

selling and disposition requirement. The same is true of financial strategies, which must only support and never lead the business.

Table 8–1 summarizes the options and how they fit with investment strategies.

Determining the Best Implementation Strategy

The best investment and management strategy in the world is of little use unless each function of the business designs and executes programs that are consistent with the strategies selected. (See Figure 8–5 for a schematic representation of implementation strategy and how it relates to other strategies.) This is so obvious that it should be unnecessary to even mention it; however, experience shows that not only

Table 8–1. The interrelationship of investment and management strategies.

Management Strategies	Invest to Grow Market or Share (More Rapidly than Competition)	Invest to Hold Position (and Maintain Moderate Market Growth)	Invest to Gradually Give Up Share and Cause Gradual Decline	Invest to Divest or Exit
Marketing-Driven Strategies				
Need/Want Identification Based on extensive market research and product market development	Very useful to grow share, create new markets or segments.	Useful to defend position by planned innovations, features, changes.	Could be useful to slow down decline— but expense may outweigh profits.	Inappropriate—too expensive.
Demand Creating Branding Advertising/promotion Training/education	Very useful to gain share, create new markets or segments.	Can be useful to defend.	Can slow down decline and possibly provide some short-term "rebirth."	Temporary tactic to attract a buyer for product line or business.
Pricing Prestige/high	Useful for creating a niche and a strong position — inappropriate for creating a "mass market" or major share gain.	Only useful if coupled with superior products. It is more a supportive than prime thrust.	Excellent way to gain short-term profits by selling off share.	Can be a way to exit, but probably will be short range.
Low/aggressive	Useful for gaining share, accelerating demand. Most effective if coupled with reducing costs.	Successful way to deter the competition.	Inappropriate. Self-deteriorating.	Inappropriate, except where it is desirable to liquidate inventories.

Distribution				
Broad	Useful to support "niche" strategies or reinforce prestige image.	Develop loyal distribution network; can be effective barrier to prevent share loss.	Pruning of distributors, focusing on only high margin or least expensive to service.	Prune rapidly or sell off to distributors who may wish to integrate backward.
Selective	Broad, expansive distribution; excellent way to aggressively expand market or grow shares.	Acquisition of independent distributors may be effective.		
Service Oriented				
Providing applications pre-sale, post-sale, and repair services	Useful to create a barrier to gain share at expense of those unable to provide service as part of the total offering.	Useful for protecting position by keeping the cost of participation high.	Useful for reducing position by cutting back or charging extra for services.	Inappropriate, except to stay in service business while exiting the product business.
Geographic/Segment Redefinition				
Expansion Contraction Selectivity	Useful to grow volume and total position by expanding offshore or into new segments with same or modified product offering.	Can be used to hold total position by changing mix of geographic and segment participation.	Prune or cut back on geographic or segments.	Selective disposition.

(continued)

Table 8-1. (Continued)

Management Strategies	Invest to Grow Market or Share (More Rapidly than Competition)	Invest to Hold Position (and Maintain Moderate Market Growth)	Invest to Gradually Give Up Share and Cause Gradual Decline	Invest to Divest or Exit
		Production-Driven Strategies		
Capacity In advance	A powerful means of gaining share in capital-intensive, long cycle businesses.	A means of providing a barrier to protect position. Keeps capital requirements high.	Inappropriate to add. Selective reduction could make sense.	Inappropriate.
Utilization	Inappropriate. Don't worry about high utilization.	Excellent way to increase profits. Could be risky if competitors add capacity and price to fill it.	Excellent way to harvest and maximize profits.	Exceeding the optimum level may assist exit.
Process Innovation	Could be effective way to maintain a strong position.	Could create a barrier to profit/defend.	Inappropriate.	Inappropriate.
Efficiency Automation	Risky. May lock you into a process inappropriate for growth. Reduces flexibility.	Automate to reduce costs and increase productivity.	Selective automation if harvest is gradual.	Inappropriate.

Supply				
Assurance				
Material substitution	Selective substitution if it doesn't inhibit growth. Backward integration too soon is inappropriate.	Excellent means of increasing productivity and decreasing costs.	Selective, but may be too costly.	Inappropriate.
Deployment				
Readiness to serve				
Warehousing				
Open stock	High levels of readiness may be critical to success of other strategies—like need identification, demand creation, innovation—but can also be means of gaining share in itself.	Normally a supportive rather than a prime strategy. May closely tie with an overall efficiency-cost-reduction strategy. Open stock can be a driver to hold share in a quality niche.	Reduced readiness may be a way to liquidate share.	Inappropriate.

Product-Driven Strategies

Leadership	Excellent way to increase both market and share. Can include leapfrog, features evolution, or standardization.	Excellent means of keeping cost of participating high as well as expensive to gain share.	Selective features and standardization can be helpful.	Inappropriate.
Quick Follow	Can be useful to capitalize on another competitor's move to develop a new market. Can be risky.	If properly timed can be effective in holding share.	Inappropriate.	Inappropriate.

(continued)

Table 8-1. (Continued)

Management Strategies	Invest to Grow Market or Share (More Rapidly than Competition)	Invest to Hold Position (and Maintain Moderate Market Growth)	Invest to Gradually Give Up Share and Cause Gradual Decline	Invest to Divest or Exit
Slow Follow	Inappropriate, unless usually strong in another area such as cost or marketing.	Inappropriate and risky, unless innovation is less critical than other factors.	Appropriate.	Inappropriate.
No Follow	Inappropriate.	Inappropriate.	Appropriate.	Appropriate.
Financially Driven Strategies				
Terms/Conditions Barter	Favorable terms/agreements may create a barrier or improve position.	Favorable terms/conditions may create a barrier.	Relatively unfavorable terms can increase earnings by decreasing share.	Unfavorable terms.
Leasing	Favorable and supportive to creating a barrier.	Can provide a competitive advantage.	Inappropriate.	Inappropriate.
Executive-Driven Strategies				
Acquisitions Mergers Joint Ventures	Useful to gain share and participate in new markets as well as gain access to new technologies.	Suitable to hold share by improving relative cost position or obtaining required technology, capacity, distribution.	Joint ventures or partnerships to decrease equity could be a gradual harvest.	Joint venture is a means of decreasing equity and gradually exiting.

must it be mentioned, but it must be properly planned and reviewed. Management can't assume that its engineering, manufacturing, or marketing executives will stop what they are doing and automatically design programs that closely fit management's chosen strategy. This is even more vital if you intend to *segment your business* and to adopt different strategies for each segment. Functional managers and organizations will continue to repeat their past programs and will not think about changing unless they are given guidelines and direction.

Let's first identify what the key strategic functional decisions are; how they will vary, depending on whether you plan to grow, hold, or harvest; and how this growth, defense, or harvest will take place. Since there are 45 viable combinations of management and investment strategies, I can't cover them all. But a few examples will help demonstrate that there are significant differences among them.

Key Business-Related Engineering Decisions

Engineering executives and their staff influence those strategic decision areas that must be properly synchronized with the investment and management strategies. These decision areas include: the scope and depth of talent and areas of expertise; the nature of the response that they will evoke; the position they will seek in the market; the level of exclusivity and proprietariness; and, finally, the type and location of facilities and equipment.

Scope and Depth

The technical organization of any business can provide a variety of skills and talents. It can have its own basic scientific research staff; it can rely on others' scientific work and dedicate its efforts to the applications of these findings; it can permit others to do the application while concentrating its own efforts on product designs and manufacturing engineering; or it can merely be a specifier and adapter of others' work. Thus, you can have a full array of engineering disciplines, or you can concentrate on a few—or even just one.

There isn't a simple formula for what you should or shouldn't offer—that will depend on the strategies you have selected. If you wish to be an innovator of revolutionary new concepts and approaches, you will most likely require a full scope and considerable depth in almost all areas. If, however, you aim at growing by aggressive pricing or promotion, you may need only design and specification talents. If you are harvesting, you may even get away with little or no engineering staff at all.

Response

A second strategic decision relates to your anticipated response to competitive conditions. Will you have a rapid response, a deliberate and slow one, or even no response at all? This is a requirement of your investment and management strategies. If you wish to develop a new market or to increase share, then you must respond quickly and skillfully to customer needs—this is particularly true in high-technology businesses. The nature of your response will also vary: Will you help in applications, developing support systems or software, installing, assuring proper operation, fixing, or adapting? Each will require different skills and different expense levels.

Image and Reputation Desired

What kind of image do you wish to project in the marketplace? Do you wish to be known as the innovator or as the follower? Again, this must be carefully tied to your total market strategy, and it can be vital to your strategy's successful implementation.

Exclusivity and Sufficiency

Related to both response and image is your desired level of proprietariness and exclusivity: Do you wish to have a unique, patent-protectable position, or will it suffice just to be one of the crowd? How long would you like to have your leadership position? This will be determined in part by your industry and your competitors, but it should also be consciously evaluated and reviewed in light of investment and management decisions. Harvesting will require only minimal exclusivity or none at all. Innovation, especially of a revolutionary nature, may demand considerable exclusivity and protection; in fact, if you can develop a long-term competitive barrier, then it may not even be worth pursuing the innovative thrust. Promotional-based strategies may require only enough exclusivity to convince the customer that you have something unique.

Funding. The decision about exclusivity enables you to determine the degree and nature of funding. You must decide where the funds will come from. Will you seek external funding from the government or from partners? If you do, you will reduce your ability to be exclusive and to have a proprietary position. Government funds require that your output become publicly known and be available to others. Partnership or joint development also inhibits exclusivity and, in fact, may create a competitor as well as a partner.

Internal funding is more consistent with exclusivity, and there are several alternatives: You can use funds generated from other products, or you can use overall corporate funds. In either case you are assuming risk but protecting the proprietary nature of your output. Pricing-, promotional-, and capacity-utilization-based strategies may be easily funded internally, whereas nw innovations, applications, and process improvements may require external funding.

Facilities and Equipment

The final decision area deals with facilities: Will you have your engineering talent concentrated in one corporate or division location, or should it be closely linked to the specific business? IBM, for example, has labs located throughout the world, whereas Philips has its facilities concentrated in Holland. This decision must be coupled with the response, flexibility, exclusivity, and funding decisions you previously made. The resulting answer will either encourage or inhibit your strategic success.

The Business-Related Engineering Strategy: A Synthesis

To illustrate the total concept, let's review the engineering strategies that may be most appropriate for *two* different investment and management strategies.

Growth-via-Revolutionary-Design Strategy

This strategy means that you plan to grow in advance of demand and possibly even to create an entirely new demand and market.

Scope. This may demand a full line of technical talents, beginning with basic research and moving through application research, advanced engineering, and design engineering.

Response. Obviously you must be first in concept or at least first with proven product or application.

Image. Your product must be differentiated or possibly customized.

Funding. The kind of funding you choose may not be critical, but it must be sufficient to permit the company to move through the entire cycle. If you use external funding, it must permit you to protect your position.

Sufficiency and exclusivity. Having a proprietary, protectable position is vital, but if it is easy to replicate or follow, then the total strategy makes no sense. At times, licensing from a small, noncompetitive company can suffice.

Facilities. Corporate funding, direction, and specialization may be enough to do the job. A design revolution takes a long-term corporate commitment.

Defend-via-Promotion Strategy

Scope. Basic and applied research and advanced engineering are luxuries you probably can't afford, but you will need the ability to design or to specify designs so that you will have a competitive product.

Response. Quick and reluctant following is most appropriate here. Lead only if it is opportunistic to do so—it isn't worth the investment.

Image. Choose the reputation of a standardizer, but maintain sufficient quality to sustain the image you are trying to create.

Fund your project in any way that you can—you will differentiate on the basis of perceived or created image.

Sufficiency and exclusivity. Adaptation of others' products, or even licensing, will suffice. Being exclusive and protective will only add unnecessary costs.

Your facilities should be small and should fit your business needs. Specialization is probably a luxury. Generalized facilities for creating perceived differences are enough.

Thus, you can see that the investment and management strategy decisions that you have made will influence the engineering programs, which in turn will influence the size of the budget, the kind of people you will hire, the level of commitment you will demand, and the size of your engineering staff. Growth via revolutionary design will require a sizable commitment, large budgets, a large number of specialized talents, and sufficient facilities. This has been the traditional thrust of Du Pont, which has tried to design new products in magnitudes sufficient to create new markets and businesses. It has had a large commitment, spending millions of dollars over long periods of time, and as a result Du Pont labs are worldwide leaders in chemistry and chemical engineering.

Manufacturing Decisions

Companies that elect to produce their own products must also be sure that their key manufacturing decisions fit their investment and management strategies. They must determine how well the following factors fit into their total strategy:

Facilities and programs
Capacity requirements
Desired flexibility
Degree of sufficiency
Productivity programs
Logistics

Facilities

The size, location, ownership, and degree of specialization of facilities can mean the difference between successful and unsuccessful implementation. Some companies elect to have one large, wholly owned, generalized manufacturing facility; others prefer small, leased, specialized facilities. The first lends itself to hold and defend manufacturing- and process-driven strategies; the second is best suited to growth-by-innovation and marketing-based strategies.

Capacity

You must decide the critical level and purpose of capacity: Are you going to relate it to demand or merely break even? Growth strategies may require a willingness to accept low utilization, whereas harvesting will emphasize high utilization. You may also choose to have access to added capacity on a leased or contract basis.

Flexibility

Will your manufacturing system be rigid, semiflexible, or highly flexible? Will the flexibility emphasize labor or equipment? There have been numerous cases in which a company was unable to respond to a growth opportunity or even to a self-developed innovation because its own manufacturing system wasn't able to adapt to the new market or to product needs. In the early stages of a product's life cycle, flexibility is vital, although the mature stages may be better suited to a nonflexible system.

Degree of Sufficiency

Being integrated or having long-term supply commitments or large stockpiles of materials may be better for some investment and management alternatives than for others. If you are harvesting over a long period of time and are emphasizing efficiency, you may prefer to have a low degree of integration and to rely on stockpiling. If, however, you wish to defend your position and to emphasize manufacturing efficiency and cost, then you would do better to have long-term contracts or even to own the suppliers. If you are using repair and maintenance service as the driver, then it is critical to have either a significant supply or the ability to rapidly produce the required part or component.

Productivity

Must you be more productive than competitive, or will it suffice to "equal" the industry average? How will your productivity be obtained, and what will it substitute for? Will it replace flexibility or sufficiency or even quality? These are strategic issues that should be resolved, and the decision should be checked against the overall strategy. Obviously productivity needs to complement some strategic options more than it does others. There is evidence that it should be considered in all situations, but even so, it can reduce the viability of some options. For example, if you wish to be the reputed service or applications leader, then it may be inappropriate for you to emphasize improving productivity. The customer's needs and expectations must be primary and, if you become too cost-conscious, you may decrease your service, and thereby abort your driving force.

How you decide to reach your productivity targets will also vary and will influence the results you get. If you attempt to replace workers by automated equipment, you may discourage rather than encourage good service. This is even more apparent in the innovation mode, because innovation doesn't conform to a precise schedule. Thus, if you were to set up such a strict schedule aimed at increasing production or at being the productive leader, you may discourage the development of the very innovation that will ultimately lead to growth.

Logistics

Logistics deals with the movement of goods to the distributor or end user. It involves decisions about whether you need to have your own trucks, ships, and trains, or whether it is satisfactory to rely on commercial transportation. In common terms, this is the "traffic" function. If you are aiming at defending your position by means of a unique service capability, it may be vital to have your own trucks and, in some cases, even planes. Control over these means of transportation can be the difference between success and failure.

Again, I would like to review how a manufacturing strategy can vary from one strategic alternative to another.

Growth-via-Revolutionary-Design Strategies

The manufacturing *facilities* will at first be small, close to the market, and customized to the specific product. An existing owned facility or a leased plant is likely to be the initial place of operations.

Capacity utilization isn't that critical: If it is low, it really shouldn't be a matter of concern.

Flexibility is vital. You may have to radically change the manufacturing process and, if you get locked in too soon, the innovation may fail. Since people are normally more flexible, your operation will more likely be people-intensive, or it will use flexible, reprogrammable computers.

Sufficiency. Rely on vendors and don't overcommit yourself or integrate too soon. Again, flexibility is an important concept.

Productivity. Don't emphasize efficiency or cost too soon.

Logistics. Input may be more critical than output. Since the product is unique, it isn't vital for you to have complete control over the logistics.

Defend-via-Promotion Strategies

Large, owned, and generalized *facilities* will probably suffice. It is most crucial to tie your facilities to the desired image you are trying to project.

Capacity. Promotion should be aimed at "load leveling" the facilities. This means that you would like a consistently high level of utilization, rather than wild fluctuations in your use of capacity.

Moderate to low *flexibility* will be satisfactory. You should key your promotion to suit the process, not the other way around. Emphasis on equipment is preferable to emphasis on labor.

Sufficiency is critical. You must be sure that you can deliver what you promise. It makes no sense to promote heavily and build demand, unless you can produce. If this means having your own source of supply, then get it. If it can be achieved by long-term contracts or stockpiling, then select the alternative that has the lowest cost.

Be sure that your *productivity* level can at least meet that of the competition. Emphasize either labor or machinery, depending on cost and profit impact.

In *logistics,* be sure that you have the resources to meet the demand that you have created.

Thus, I have tried to illustrate that among manufacturing strategies there are differences that are influenced by investment and management strategies. In both cases the kinds of skills, resources, commitment, and finances will vary. Many companies have been unable to be innovators or promoters, because their manufacturing was inappropriate or they were unable to deliver what was required.

Marketing Decisions

Marketing decisions must determine product management and planning, distribution, sales, service, intelligence, readiness to serve, promotions, and pricing.

Product Management and Planning

Determining whether you will be a leader or quick follower or slow follower is a decision that requires the input and careful execution of both engineering and marketing. If leadership has been identified as being critical to success, then both engineering and marketing must respond: Engineering must determine the internal viability of such an approach, and marketing must evaluate the customer's needs and wants. In addition, you must make a decision as to the scope and depth of your product line—for instance, will you need to have a complete line and to offer components, subsystems, and total systems? Distribution-based strategies normally require a complete and in-depth line, whereas pricing or promotional strategies will enable you to be more selective. Engineering, marketing, and manufacturing must be carefully integrated, and all must be geared to the successful implementation of the investment and management strategy.

Distribution Strategy

Industries vary in the number of steps between the manufacturer and the user. In some cases there may be a wholesaler, a jobber, and a retailer in the cycle, whereas in others there may only be a retailer or even a direct line from manufacturer to user. The issue is whether you must increase or decrease the existing number of steps, or accept the present number.

Next, you should decide whether you wish to have distributors with a long-term, exclusive commitment. For instance, automobile dealers must be willing to sign long-term agreements and to represent only one brand of cars. You must also determine if the dealers or distributors will be specialists or generalists and whether you want them to provide service.

In some cases, it is critical to have dealers or distributors who are product experts and are willing to help the customer select the product, use the equipment, and even repair and maintain it. This is particularly critical in the case of the growth-via-innovation strategy where, since the product may be unknown, it would be desirable to have the dealer or distributor back the product, carry your line exclusively, and give you a medium- to long-term commitment. This may also be the case if you sell your product to another manufacturer who in turn incorporates it into his product. (These manufacturers are called original equipment manufacturers, commonly referred to as OEMs.)

On the other hand, a strategy driven by promotional protection may have different requirements. For instance, since you plan to maintain user loyalty and acceptance of your product, the dealer or distributor is less critical. Therefore, you can succeed with generalists who have low to medium commitment, carry multiple brands, have little knowledge of the product, and prefer to offer as little service as possible. This may be viable because the user is likely to be knowledgeable, and if he needs help, he is likely to turn to you.

Sales Strategy

The kind of distributor you select and its role in the sale will influence your sales organization: Will you have your own sales force exclusively, or will you have a mixture of agents and representatives in addition to your own? What kinds of skills will you require? Technical, problem-solving, personal selling, and promotional skills should be considered and the priorities selected. Will you train your own salesmen or hire those with past experience? Will training be in depth, or will each salesman be left to learn on his own?

Organization and rewards should also be determined. Will you organize around geography, product, applications, or some combination of these factors? And what about rewards? Salary, salary and small commission, small salary and large commission, no salary and larger commission—these are some of the options. These decisions will vary with the investment and management strategies that you select.

Growth via innovation. This strategy will require highly qualified, trained, knowledgeable salespeople who can work with the user and distributor and who must know all aspects of the product. This may mean that you organize around applications, and that training in depth and in advance with periodic updates can be vital. Finally, since growth means improved position, you will reward your staff on applications and increased sales but as an incentive you will probably rely primarily on salary with a share-based bonus or commission.

Defense via promotion. This approach has different needs. You may have some of your own salespeople, but you may also rely on agents and representatives, who will not have to be experts and for whom training will be necessary only when new models or applications are being stressed. Maintaining share is the goal, and margin should be stressed. As incentives, commissions will probably weigh more heavily than salary.

Service Strategies

Products require some form of service, including pre-sale, applications, instruction, maintenance, repair, and upgrading. These services can be offered for a variety of reasons. You can offer them to differentiate your product and thus enable you to grow or to hold share. Normally the cost of these services will be bundled (included in the product purchasing price) or will be offered purely on a cost/minimal-charge basis. Another reason for offering service is to assure the customer that you are serious about the product and that you are concerned about his problems—this will also serve to enhance sales. But you can also make service an income/profit center. (In this case, it is unbundled and is aimed at income rather than sales.) If this approach is handled creatively, you can optimize sales and income, but this is difficult and may turn out to be counterproductive.

You must make decisions about the purpose of service, and these will guide you in your decisions about the scope and pricing of the services. If you are likely to bundle for sales, then offer full scope and charge nothing or charge only for expenses. If you will unbundle for income, then charge for profit and only offer services that have high income potential.

The final decision will be aimed at determining how much control you will have over the service. This will mean a choice between having your own service, franchising service, or merely providing parts and guidance to your customers.

Growth via innovation. In the early stages of a new product you must have strong service. This will mean that service is bundled, covers the complete range from pre- to post-sales service, and is offered by trained, skilled, company-managed or franchised servicemen—in short, complete, low-priced, and controlled service.

Defense via promotion. In this case service is less critical, and the options are more extensive. Normally, it will suffice to offer service for a profit. Only those service offerings that are absolutely necessary (because they are unavailable anywhere else) or that bring in profits should be initiated. Sufficiency and control should also be geared toward profitability and toward meeting competitive standards. You must offer only what is necessary to defend and support the image that you are trying to project.

Intelligence Strategies

Executives must become more sensitive to the need to anticipate situations and to convert data into intelligence. Some strategies require you to focus on the future; others demand more emphasis on the present. Similarly, you can either rely on existing information or go out and retrieve "firsthand" information. Existing information based on written documentation is called secondary data; firsthand information is called primary data. But data about what? Will you emphasize customer, competitive, or governmental data?

If you plan to grow with a revolutionary new product, then you can't rely on existing secondary data, since none exist. You must seek out customers' data about their satisfaction with current products or services, and then determine the likely acceptance for the product you intend to offer. Furthermore, you are interested primarily in the future, not merely in the present. Finally, competitive and customer data are vital, especially if you intend to substitute your product for an established one.

However, defending via promotion is less intelligence-sensitive. You can probably rely on existing and secondary data to anticipate changes and avoid surprises. You can live with data more oriented toward the present than to the future and aimed at tracking competitive moves.

Readiness-to-Serve Strategies

This decision must be correlated with manufacturing as well as with investment and management strategies. It focuses on the desired inventory that you will have on hand. In an earlier chapter, I mentioned that service levels can be differentiators and can thus be the leading thrusts of a strategy.

Some companies aim at being overly and distinctly responsive, whereas others seem to have little or no concern with this. Responsiveness can be expressed in percentages and time: Do you wish to respond with 80% of the items in a week, or 70% in three days, or 90% in a day? The time period is strongly influenced by the nature of the product, and the percentage is related to your desired competitive position. Will you equal, exceed, or lag behind the competition? The more you decide to lead, the more control you are likely to require. Thus, you will require your own warehousing and inventory, or the ability to manufacture the product rapidly to order.

To return to this illustration, growth via innovation will require a leadership position. Rapid response (faster than your competition) of product and spare parts will demand that you have your own warehousing or inventory. You can rely on distributors for stock and, if you delay, you may irreparably damage your reputation. Defense via promotion can also be demanding in this regard: You must be able to meet customer and competitive requirements, but you may find that the control is less in your hands and more in the hands of the distributor or of other intermediaries. Other intermediaries may be original equipment manufacturers (OEMs) who sell your product as an integral part of theirs.

Promotion Strategies

Having the best product in large quantities and manufacturing it in quality-oriented plants is inadequate if the customer doesn't know that it exists. Strangely, this fact isn't recognized by many executives. How will you let the customer know what you are offering and how it compares with his other alternatives? Will you rely on the written or spoken word? Will the message be periodic or continuous? How will your expenditures compare with those of your key competitors and with the industry averages?

Growth via product innovation will require a strong pull strategy to support it. This means that you must aggressively inform people about your new, revolutionary product. This may require on-site demonstrations and promotional materials that explain the wonders of your new product so as to encourage the user to at least try it. This is especially true if you want customers to switch from their current products. In that case, your advertising budget must be significant, and it must exceed the outlays of your major competitors. Defending by promotion will require siilar programs: By definition, you must aggressively publicize your product and brand. Your message must be strong and consistent. This is the means that you have selected to create a "perceived" differentiation, and if you fail to spend more than the industry average, then you aren't really using this management strategy.

Pricing Strategies

You must decide on your pricing strategy and be sure that it is tied to your management strategy. There are three key decisions. First, you must determine your position in the marketplace—will you be the price leader or follower? If you intend to follow, how rapidly? If you want to lead, will you lead upward or downward?

Second, what will be the basis of your pricing? Will you base it on cost (manufacturing or total cost), on desired gross or contribution margin, on perceived or customer value, on anticipated inflation, or on competitors? These decisions can influence the management strategy that you select, but they can also affect the success of implementation. The basis of your pricing decisions must be consistent with your total strategy.

Third, you must coordinate price with terms and conditions. You can actually lead in price and follow in terms. This is the discounter's strategy—low price but no credit or extended payments ("low price but cash and carry"). Or you can maintain high prices but offer attractive credit terms. This is often followed by the prestige retailer who favors high quality and high price but extended, low-interest credit.

Innovative growth demands high, controlled pricing based on "perceived value," using terms and conditions rather than direct pricing. In this case you want the price to reinforce your image of quality, innovation, and uniqueness. Customers normally equate these characteristics with high or premium prices, and it is often better to offer attractive terms than premium prices. Defending by promotion may demand a different thrust in which you will most likely price on cost or margin. Your prices will be competitive, but you are more likely to be a reluctant follower than a leader. Terms will be tied to price and support.

Overall Assessment of Implementation Strategy

The message should be clear: Functional and supporting strategies must fit the total business strategy—which includes both the investment and management strategies—and be internally consistent. (See Tables 8–2 and 8–3 for detailed overviews of the various aspects of implementation strategy outlined in this chapter.) For instance, the engineering decision to lead, follow, or be a customized, differentiated producer must fit in with both the manufacturing strategy and the product planning activities of marketing. If you decide to lead, your manufacturing must be flexible and product development must determine what it takes to lead. But suppose that you wish to "quick follow"; then your manufacturing systems must be flexible or you must have the means to quickly make or obtain product. Your line may be limited at first and be more extensive later. Distribution decisions must fit in with your readiness-to-serve and manufacturing decisions. Furthermore, your productivity thrust will affect both your pricing and your ability to lead or to respond rapidly to competitors' moves.

Table 8–2. An overview of various implementation strategies for two different investment and management strategies.

	Growth via Product Innovation	*Defense via Promotion*
Engineering		
SCOPE	Full scope from basic research to design	Limited scope—primarily design or specification
POSITION	Leader	Quick or reluctant follower
RESPONSE	Rapidly differentiated, possibly customized	Standardized/at own pace or to meet competition
FUNDING	*Internal*—preferred *External*—only if you can protect	Any way that you can
EXCLUSIVITY	Proprietary, protectable	Adaptation or licensed from someone else
FACILITIES	Corporate, specialized—total commitment	Business generalized; customer responsive
Manufacturing		
FACILITIES	Small, close to market, self-owned	Large, generalized, owned or leased
CAPACITY	As much as possible, without sacrificing innovation and quality	"Load leveling," constantly high utilization
FLEXIBILITY	High—using either people or easy-to-reprogram computers	Moderate to low
SUFFICIENCY	Flexibility—not critical	Sufficiency is critical
PRODUCTIVITY	Don't emphasize cost too soon	Ability to be "least-cost" for contingency response
LOGISTICS	Some concern about incoming traffic	Critical—to assure proper response

(continued)

Table 8–2. (Continued)

	Growth via Product Innovation	*Defense via Promotion*
Marketing		
PRODUCT MANAGEMENT	Lead, limited scope initially, differentiate	Reluctant follower, full scope and standardized
DISTRIBUTION	Specialized, service, exclusive long-term commitment	Generalized, nonservice, multiple brand, low–medium commitment
SALES	Highly qualified, trained, knowledgeable, applications, training, owned—salary and some commission	Not experts, some training, order takers, commission
SERVICE	Strong for sales Bundled Trained, skilled	For profit Unbundled
INTELLIGENCE	Customer focused Future Primary	Competitively focused Avoid surprises Secondary
READINESS	Rapid/anticipatory Controlled	Meet competition Intermediaries
PROMOTION	Strong pull Aggressive Above average	Strong Aggressive Above average
PRICING	High Controlled Perceived value Terms if necessary	Meet competition Cost/margin Compatible terms

Table 8–3. An overview of key business strategy implementation decisions.

	Engineering	Manufacturing	Marketing
SCOPE AND DEPTH	Basic sciences / Applied research / Advanced engineering / Design engineering / Specification	**FACILITIES**: Size / Location / Ownership / Degree of specialization	**PRODUCT MANAGEMENT/ PLANNING**: Standing / Scope / Depth
		CAPACITY: Demand vs. breakeven	**DISTRIBUTION**: Steps; Service / Commitment / Specialization / Exclusivity
RESPONSE	Rapid / Deliberate / Slow / None	**FLEXIBILITY**: Rigid, semi–full flexibility / Labor vs. equipment	**SALES**: Type; Reward / Skills; Training / Organization
POSITION	Innovator / Follower	**DEGREE OF SUFFICIENCY**: Integrated, stockpiled, purchase / Raw material / Components / Spare parts	**SERVICE**: Scope; Purpose / Sufficiency/Control; Bundling
EXCLUSIVITY/ SUFFICIENCY	High, medium, low / Own, partners, licensed		**INTELLIGENCE**: Time horizon / Type; Emphasis
			READINESS: Rapidity; Control / Approach/Focus
FUNDING	Internal / External	**PRODUCTIVITY**: Standing / Approach	**PROMOTION**: Standing / Emphasis / Continuity
FACILITIES AND EQUIPMENT	Centralized vs. decentralized / Generalist vs. specialist	**LOGISTICS**: Incoming vs. outgoing / Approach	**PRICING**: Basis; Standing / Terms/Conditions

9

The Final Steps

ALTHOUGH you now have a strategy for each segment and a set of guidelines for implementing those strategies, you must develop plans. In this chapter I will describe what you do after you have formulated guidelines. This includes:

1. Checking the guidelines against your current strategy.
2. Surfacing differences and determining what must be changed to successfully implement your strategy.
3. Developing the correct method of using your strengths and correcting your deficiencies.
4. Reviewing your total strategy and testing for its overall viability.
5. Determining the type of management required.
6. Making sure that all business systems support the idea of management by strategy.

Checking Your Guidelines Against Reality
Through a "Growth via Innovation" Strategy

Suppose that you review each segment to determine how the guidelines fit the current strategy and programs being executed and determine that there isn't a sufficient match. For example, in the last chapter I described the engineering, manufacturing, and marketing programs that are most likely to help you gain share; I called this program "revolutionary product innovation," or "growth via product innovation." I shall use this as an example of how you can check the results against the guidelines that you have set up, and thereby evaluate your success or failure.

Engineering Strategy

The guidelines call for the full scope of engineering activity, from basic research to design engineering, all the while emphasizing real and perceived technological leadership. The organization should aim at providing customized or differentiated products, and it should be able to respond rapidly to customer needs and to competitors' moves. Funding should be internal so that the company can develop and protect a proprietary position. Corporate commitment should be long-range. Laboratories should be dedicated to developing the innovation. In short, with this approach you are seeking a protectable breakthrough.

However, when you review your engineering strategies and programs, you conclude that you don't have a full range: You don't have the basic research, but have instead focused on applications engineering that is aimed at developing a leadership position. Differentiation and some customization is being executed, but you have relied on external funding, primarily governmental funds. Because of the governmental funding, your corporate commitment is erratic, and much of the work is being done in multipurpose laboratories. Thus, you have noted gaps in the scope, funding, and nature of your technical facilities. But what does this mean? Must you fix it, or can you live with these deficiencies?

An examination of the competition shows that the lack of basic research is not a problem, but that none of the competitors has basic research capability: Everyone relies on the research done in universities and in nonprofit labs, and they all concentrate on applied engineering to create a barrier. So, there is no need to panic or even to change your plans: The guidelines don't describe your needs, and you can explain why they don't.

The funding issue, however, does indicate a problem. The use of governmental funds enables the competitors to build off your research and developments, since the results are in the "public domain." Furthermore, two of your key competitors have used internal funding and have a more protectable position—this means that you are violating the guidelines, whereas the competition is adhering to them.

But suppose that you are willing to live with the lack of basic research and with the use of generalized labs, but believe that you must get more internal and less external funding. This will require more corporate commitment, and you must ask yourself why commitment has been low and what you can do to increase it. Again, you must examine the cause and make a determination: Perhaps you haven't told management why this program is so important and how it can rebuild or strengthen your image. Thus, you will make this a key "upward" communications objective.

For an assessment of engineering strategy in this situation, see Table 9–1.

Manufacturing Strategy

THE RECOMMENDATION OF THE GUIDELINES

The guidelines recommend that your production facilities be small, dedicated, and responsive to customer needs. This means that flexibility is more important than productivity and capacity utilization. It will require sufficient, but not more than sufficient, materials and logistics. You don't want too much backward integration or a management so concerned with costs that it will ignore competitors' actions or customers' requirements. Obviously this is a matter of degree, since you

Table 9–1. Evaluation of engineering strategy.

Investment Strategy: Growth
Management Strategy: Product innovation (new features)

	Preferred Implementation	*Current Implementation*	*Actions Required*
SCOPE	Full scope from basic to design	No basic research	Accept deficiency
IMAGE	Lead	Satisfactory	Continue
RESPONSE	Rapid, differentiated, possibly customized	Being executed	Continue
FUNDING	*Internal* (preferred) *External*—if you can protect	Primarily external	Reallocate some internal funds
EXCLUSIVITY	Proprietary, protectable	Satisfactory	
FACILITIES	Corporate Specialized Total commitment	Too generalized	Get more specialized, and focus on your innovation

Assessment: Engineering is sufficiently close to strategic requirements. Merely refocus some elements.

can't afford to be so concerned with flexibility that your costs will be noncompetitive.

THE REALITY OF THE SITUATION

When you study current programs, you conclude that your strategy emphasizes large, centralized, multiproduct facilities, but that in fact, the new products are being produced on equipment normally used for volume lines. Nonflexible capacity-, productivity-, and logistics-based processes and equipment are the norm, rather than the exception.

In short, your manufacturing strategy is the *antithesis* of what is required, and it would be better suited for manufacturing efficiency and cost reduction strategies than for the one you are proposing. This is a critical problem that raises questions about the viability of the overall strategy. You conclude, and I would agree, that you must change your current manufacturing strategy. This will require moving to a plant with processes, management, and people that are adaptable to customer needs rather than to cost and efficiency demands. This may mean a new plant and organization, and additional corporate cash and capital.

See Table 9–2 for an overall assessment of manufacturing strategy in this situation.

OPTIONS FOR CHANGE

1. You can use the existing plant and merely allocate a part of it to this innovative product.

2. You can change the focus of the workforce and management through increased training, offering rewards, or hiring new individuals to undertake the tasks required.

3. You can subcontract the manufacturing to another company that will be more geared to flexibility and responsiveness. This would be less disruptive, but it may require a stronger control and quality-monitoring system.

4. You can joint venture with another company that already has the kind of manufacturing you require. Again, this is less disruptive but demands a new control and integration system.

5. Finally, you could acquire a company that not only has the proper manufacturing processes but can also complement your marketing and engineering efforts.

But depending on the option you select, you must reevaluate your manpower, rewards, and managerial system.

Marketing Strategies

The guidelines describe the need for a product-planning and management system that will cause the customers to consider you a leader in anticipating and meeting their needs.

Table 9–2. Evaluation of manufacturing strategy.

Investment Strategy: Growth
Management Strategy: Product innovation (new features)

	Preferred Implementation	*Current Implementation*	*Actions Required*
FACILITIES	Small, close to market, self-owned	Large, far from markets, multiproduct	
CAPACITY	As much as possible without sacrificing innovation and quality	Capacity utilization-focused	Need to change entire manufacturing strategy
FLEXIBILITY	High—using either people or reprogrammable computers	Not flexible	*Options:* 1. Separate from other products
EFFICIENCY	Enough to permit response and flexibility—no backward integration	Backward integration	2. Redirect 3. Subcontract 4. Joint venture 5. Acquire
PRODUCTIVITY	Don't emphasize cost too early	Aimed at productivity	
LOGISTICS	Some concern about incoming traffic	Both incoming and outgoing	

Assessment: Change or rethink entire strategy. Can't continue current practices and still be successful.

Distributors should be knowledgeable, specialized, and service-oriented: The stronger their loyalty to you (and your commitment to them), the more successful this strategy will be, perhaps resulting in their willingness to carry only one brand—yours.

You must also have a sales force that reinforces your distributor's offerings, assures customer satisfaction, and is deeply knowledgeable about the product, its uniqueness, and its applications. Your salespeople should be rewarded when they increase product share and total market penetration. Service supports sales and enhances customer satisfaction, from pre- to post-sales and maintenance of the product. The intelligence system is based on anticipatory, primary data, and inventory is stocked to meet customer needs. Promotion is aggressive, is backed by a sizable budget, and is geared to creating interest and excitement. Pricing should be value priced, controlled, and differentiated (terms used other than base price).

Again, you should review your current strategy. Your product planning is aimed at leadership and fits the new product thrust—hence, no change is required. Distributors are generalized and have no interest in providing service or specialized applications. Your inventory is geared toward manufacturing efficiency and isn't strong: It is common for you to run out of unusually popular items. The total organization has no dedication to readiness to serve. Promotional expenditures are below industry levels, and well below those of the leader.

Pricing and sales are consistent. Pricing is value controlled, and terms are used to differentiate. Your own sales force is trained and knowledgeable and is used to making up for the deficiencies of dealers and distributors. Another problem is service, which is unbundled and doesn't emphasize repair and maintenance to support sales. Finally, intelligence gathering uses secondary data, and monitors situations rather than anticipates new situations.

Marketing is discontinuous, with less serious changes than those required by manufacturing. Distribution, inventory, promotion, and service need to be changed. More emphasis should be put on responsiveness to customer needs and wants. This can be done in a number of ways, but the most effective means is to strengthen the programs currently being implemented. Increase the number of specialists and servicing distributors, along with your own service, and promote it aggressively. Thus, marketing modifications are needed, although they won't have to be as drastic as the changes in manufacturing.

See Table 9-3 for an overall assessment of marketing strategy in this situation.

Harvesting-via-High-Pricing Strategy

Let's contrast the needs of our growth example with those of a harvesting-via-high-pricing strategy. In this case, you have decided to trade long-term growth for short-term profits by pricing high and by not being too concerned about competitors or customers. The level of pricing premiums is tied to the degree and timing of erosion.

Engineering Strategy

Instead of full-scope leadership and long-term commitment, this strategy is geared to a minimum response. All you need is a small staff that is capable of specifying a new design, if it is absolutely necessary for a gradual harvest. It is also possible to make no response if one isn't necessary for survival during the harvest period.

Suppose, however, that you have been implementing the strategy described earlier—a composite of manufacturing efficiency and product innovation which is not integrated between the functional organizations. You will have too much staff and will be aiming at more leadership than is required. You must therefore reduce the level of commitment and staff and allocate only enough funds for harvesting.

Manufacturing Strategy

The manufacturing, however, is much closer to what is required. A large, multiproduct, efficiency-oriented process is appropriate for a harvest strategy, but it is more important to emphasize cost and efficiency than to emphasize flexibility. One area of concern may be the focus on integration: You may have more integration than you require and, instead of

Table 9–3. Evaluation of marketing strategy.

Investment Strategy: Growth
Management Strategy: Product innovation

	Preferred Implementation	*Current Implementation*	*Actions Required*
PRODUCT PLAN	Lead—anticipate customer needs	Satisfactory	No change
DISTRIBUTORS	Knowledgeable Specialized Service Long-range commitment	Generalists, no service volume orientation Generalists, no service volume orientation	Add new specialized, service-oriented personnel for this product
READINESS TO SERVE	Rapid	Low	Add more inventory, tie in with new distributors
PROMOTION	Aggressive	Minimum	Tie in with new distributors Increase pull
PRICING	Value-controlled Terms- rather than price-differentiated	Satisfactory	No change
SALES	Knowledgeable about product	Satisfactory	No change
SERVICE	Bundled Full-range	Income-oriented, unbundled	Add service and bundle for 3 years
INTELLIGENCE	Primary, anticipatory	Secondary, monitoring	No change—live with what you have

Assessment: Not a serious discontinuity. Some minor changes required.

adding to it or even maintaining the status quo, you may wish to liquidate some of it or redirect it to other business segments. Thus, the degree of change may be small.

Marketing Strategy

The emphasis on nonservicing, generalist distributors, low inventory, and a minimum level of advertising and service also fits the harvest-by-high-pricing strategy. The pricing and intelligence gathering also tie closely. The only major change is in product positioning, which must move from a "lead" to a "no follow" status.

Thus, the major change required in a harvesting-via-high-pricing strategy is in the engineering area, which actually requires cutting back and deemphasizing, whereas the growth-via-product-innovation strategy required changes in manufacturing. In the case of reducing engineering, you will require programs aimed at laying off engineering personnel and reassigning them to other components, segments, or businesses; closing or reassigning laboratories; and reducing or reallocating the engineering and technical budget. But you must be sure that your reductions in one segment won't hurt the growth or defense of another.

Reviewing the Total Strategy

After you have reviewed each segment separately and have determined what changes are required, you should review the total strategy and see if you can transfer talent from one segment to another. The diagram in Figure 9–1 is a useful way to depict your final decisions. This includes the investment and management strategies as well as the current sales and net income for each of the segments.

In this diagram, you have $410 million in sales and $19 million in pretax margin. This is a 4.6% pretax income, and 2.4% after taxes. You have over 73% of sales coming from a hold or defend segment. This accounts for 79% of your net income; $60 million of sales is derived from growth segments, which show negative income. The $50 million of sales on the harvest side is the largest income and cash generator.

Figure 9-1. A sample of a total strategy.

	Growth	Holding	Harvesting	Divestment
Product innovation	Segment A–Revolution $15 million sales $(2) million pretax margin			
Marketing		Segment B–Applications $300 million sales $15 million pretax margin	Segment C–Price $50 million sales $5 million pretax margin	
Manufacturing	Segment D–Supply $45 million sales $1 million pretax margin			
Finance				

With this insight, you can now determine how you might be able to fill the gaps that you identified. For instance, suppose you decide that you need more design engineers to execute your supply-growth strategy. Further analysis shows that the engineers unnecessary for segment C harvesting can fit your requirements—thus, you don't have to lay them off, but can transfer them. The manufacturing staff and equipment

Figure 9-2. A total strategy that may not be viable.

	Growth	Holding	Harvesting	Divestment

Product Innovation	Segment A—
	Revolution
	$20 million
	  sales
	$2 million
	  pretax
	   margin			

Marketing		Segment D—
		Service
		$150 million
		  sales
		$15 million
		  pretax
		   margin		

Production	Segment B—
	Capacity
	$15 million
	  sales
	$2 million
	  pretax
	   margin			

Finance	Segment C—
	Leasing
	$50 million
	  sales
	$(5) million
	  pretax
	   margin			

that you have assigned to segment A doesn't have to hire new people, but can move them to segment C. In this way you can see clearly what the overall needs are and whether the total strategy makes sense and is viable. The situation that I just illustrated has good balance and appears feasible, but this may not always be the case.

Figure 9–2 depicts an overall strategy that may not be viable, even though its individual segments seem to work well.

In this case, three segments represent $85 million in sales and a $1 million loss in pretax margin, whereas, one segment represents sales of $150 million and profits of $15 million. On the surface this also appears to be viable and, in fact, there is a balance toward growth. Nevertheless, this company needs to improve its engineering and manufacturing organizations while maintaining its marketing strengths. This may require more growth than the company can handle, particularly during the time period required: Too much growth in a short period of time is questionable.

Options for Change

As I mentioned there are a number of ways to make the required changes in strategy and even though I discussed many of these earlier, it may be useful to review them here.

If the changes call for enhancing or even maintaining skills, this can be done by:

1. Hiring new people, building new plants, or installing new, improved equipment.
2. Upgrading the people, facilities, or equipment through training, modernization, or improvements.
3. Purchasing another organization's services and abilities or subcontracting.
4. Joint venturing with another company that has the required skills.
5. Acquisition of an entire company to fill the required gaps.
6. Transferring talents from one part of your company to another.

If the changes require a reduction of skills or resources, this can be done by:

1. Transferring the talents to where they are needed.
2. Layoffs or attrition.
3. Selling talent to another company or organization that needs it.

The Role of Management in Planning and Executing Strategies

We all recognize that engineers who are required to rapidly follow and modify the designs of the innovator or leader are very different from those who are supposed to be innovators. Obviously, if you have one kind of engineer but need the other kind, this mismatch must be corrected. The same is true in manufacturing and marketing. Manufacturing professionals skilled at cost-cutting and at developing automation systems are not always suited to make innovations and create new manufacturing systems. Similarly, marketing personnel who are skilled at applications engineering, providing technical support, and selling on the basis of service rather than price, are different from those who sell best on promotion.

The same thing is true of managerial talents and skills. I would like to review the major managerial tasks and the various kinds of experiences, skills, and areas of knowledge that could make an impact on successful strategic management.

Most textbooks reduce managerial work to four categories: planning, organizing, measuring, and controlling. This book is about one phase of planning—namely, long-range strategic planning—but it is not the only kind of critical planning; there must also be short-term tactical or action planning. Some strategies put more emphasis on one than on the other, but both must be executed. Thus, planning should be reviewed in light of the selected strategy and of management's ability to execute it properly.

After the plan is developed, the manager must organize to carry it out. Some strategies require total centralization: others may require modified or total decentralization. Obviously these forms of organization may vary from one situation to another, but they must conform to the overall strategy. A plan and an organization require measurement and control. Management must decide what it wants to achieve, how to measure the results, and what rewards or punishments to parcel out.

Different Strategies and Their Requisite Management Skills

The kind of measurement and control must also conform to the strategy: You must obviously reward growth differently than you would reward stabilization or reduction. Furthermore, some strategies will demand immediate rewards; others require long-term rewards. How quickly you act in a given situation will also vary. Let's review how the various strategies will affect the kind of planning, organization, measurement, and control that you adopt.

Revolutionary product-innovation strategies will require long-term strategic planning, a strong centralized participative organization, and long-term measurement and rewards. You can't expect instant results, and you should base your rewards on your long-term business success. This kind of strategy also requires a management that understands the technology and that will know when the project isn't going to be successful. It is a risk-intensive strategy.

"Quick follow" product-innovative strategies, however, require a more balanced view and a willingness to be responsive. This means a more decentralized organization, moderate risk-taking, and rewards that are based on the ability to respond rapidly and successfully. These strategies don't require as much technical knowledge, however.

There are some who believe that technically based strategies require technically educated, experienced managers. I'm not convinced that a technical background is necessary; in fact, it may be an obstacle. This is particularly true if the technical background instills biases and impedes creativity and innovation. The successful manager needs to appreciate the problems of innovating. He or she must recognize that risk is involved, and must be supportive of the staff. Of course, there are successful entrepreneurial inventors, like Dr. Edward Land, as well as the most successful of all—Thomas Alva Edison. But these geniuses also knew when to permit the business innovators to take over.

The management skills required for marketing-based strategies are significantly different from those required for technically based strategies. But it also differs depending on the kind of marketing strategy you choose. Service-, application-, and distribution-based strategies require more strategic planning than demand-creation and pricing strategies. This also means a willingness to allow longer-range horizons and measurements. Decentralized and participative management appears to be appropriate for all the alternatives, but pricing may require tighter, more centralized control. Both demand creation and pricing require more rapid decision making and better market responsiveness. There is also a need for more precise timing in implementation.

It appears that a marketing background also supports this kind of strategy. Note that I said *marketing,* not sales. Pricing and promotional strategies are mostly sales-oriented, but even in these situations the best salesman may make the worst manager. What is critical is sound business skills, supported by an intuitive feel for the market and for the key customer needs.

Production-focused strategies also vary, and appear to have different management needs. Capacity, process, and supply strategies that aim at positioning the company against future uncertainties often require long-term strategic thinking and planning, whereas strategies aimed at utilization and rapid response are more tactical, shorter term, and implementation oriented. Deployment strategies are medium term and implementation oriented. These strategies also influence the kind of organization you will need. Centralized, top-down, tightly controlled organizations are preferable, since you are attempting to optimize the total manufacturing and logistical system. If, however, you are required to respond rapidly to supply shortages, factory-filling moves, or changes in processes, then some delegated but supervised decentralization may help. In long-cycle businesses, the measurements must be geared to the long range.

Do you need a manufacturing-oriented manager to implement this kind of strategy? In this case, I believe that it is helpful and even preferable. A successful manufacturing professional is usually systematic, disciplined, and interested in optimization—these are the kinds of skills and characteristics that are best suited for this kind of strategy. These characteristics can all be found in accountants, lawyers, and engineers, but the combination of these skills and managerial know-how is highly desirable. The manufacturing professional is therefore a good candidate to implement manufacturing-based strategies.

Financial- and executive-based strategies also support centralization over decentralization and long-term measurements over short-term ones. Both of these strategies are built on the corporation's lifeblood—its cash and capital. Hence, it is important to have a long-term strategic view rather than a short-term opportunistic perspective. In addition, these strategies require managements—such as those of lending institutions and governments—that can work with outsiders.

Do you need to be a banker or a financial wizard? Not necessarily, although you do need to understand finance and the financial implications of your decisions. You must be a realist and have the ability to assess the financial risks involved. Good instincts about the options are probably critical.

You should also compare your *current* strategy and the resources of your total management system to the guidelines that you have set for yourself. If you find that you need a long-term, high-risk, tightly controlled, decisive management and a strategy requiring capacity in advance of demand but if you find that you have the exact opposite, then you must carry out an extensive reexamination. Do you believe that the guidelines are correct? Do you wish to change the investment and management strategies? Can your management system be modified to meet the minimum requirements? In short, you must be objective and realistic and not be lulled into a false sense of security.

See Table 9–4 for an overview of how investment and management strategies influence the type of management, the planning system, organizational structure, measurements, rewards, and controls. I have outlined three strategies which can serve as a guideline in the same manner as implementation strategies. Note that the type of management varies considerably, as do the planning emphasis, measurements, and rewards. The organizational structure is quite similar. Centralized controls are appropriate for all three, though the controls are focused on different measures. Since there are 45 different combinations of investment and management strategies, it is impossible to describe them all, but it is important to evaluate the impact of each combination on the organization and measurement systems.

Critical Factors in Successful Planning

There are several critical success factors that must be met in order to have an effective strategic management and planning system. Several of these have already been discussed, including having the proper skills, measurements, and management. In addition, however, there must be a recognition that planning is a means, not an end. There must also be the proper level of involvement and commitment by the chief executive officer, as well as a good match between budgeting, resource allocation systems, and strategic planning.

Factor I: Planning Is a Means, Not an End

Implementation strategy links investment and management strategy decisions to action plans. But it is a means, not an end. Most planners seem to forget this fact. They consider themselves professionals and, like most professionals, become so enamored of the technology of planning that they lose sight of their true goal—helping the organization select, implement, and achieve realistic objectives and goals. Planning is a means to help management communicate and lead. This point must be kept in mind.

Factor II: Involvement of the Chief Executive Officer

All the activities I have described require the support, involvement, and long-range commitment of the chief executive officer and of the board of directors. I mention the latter

Table 9–4. Impact of investment and management

Business Systems and Characteristics	Growth by Product Innovation	Hold or Defend by Manufacturing Efficiency	Harvest by High Pricing
Characteristics of top management	Growth oriented Understanding of technology to degree necessary to allocate sufficient resources Willing to assume risk Ability to manage creatively	Profit oriented Manufacturing/cost/financial controls background Willing to take decisive actions if profits are not being achieved	Profit and cash flow oriented Understanding and ability to operate with small organization Willing to prune and cut back
The planning system	Long-term strategic planning Strong emphasis on customer, competition, and technology Strong need for contingency plans	Medium- to long-term strategic and operational planning emphasis on internal resource planning Monitoring of external factors influencing cost	Short term Reactive Monitor to avoid major surprises and little more

because legal and judicial actions are increasingly becoming the liability of the board. As the board becomes liable, its members will act less as absentee managers and more as decision makers. The chief executive officer and the board must be demanding and have realistic expectations about planning.

strategies on business systems.

Business Systems and Characteristics	Growth by Product Innovation	Hold or Defend by Manufacturing Efficiency	Harvest by High Pricing
Organization	Centralized with participation from functional staffs, especially marketing and engineering Possible use of matrix organization	Centrally controlled with a cost reduction and efficiency orientation Functionally organized	Centralized Small Functionally oriented
Measurement and rewards	Long-term profitability Short-term market growth Specific milestones and goals to monitor progress	Profitability oriented Emphasis on return on investment and equity	Short term Reward on cash flow
Controls	Centralized Ability to trigger change and execute contingency response if and when needed	Centralized Geared to total cost Ability to move rapidly if productivity is moving in wrong direction	Centralized Geared to least cost Ability to exit if required

They shouldn't expect miracles, nor should they have such low expectations that planning hardly exists.

But what should chief executive officers do? What roles should they play? First of all, chief executive officers should demand that their operating managers and staff provide the data and analyses necessary to make proper investment decisions for each business and, in some cases, for the critical segments within the business. They alone know the extent of their resources, and must allocate them. They must decide where the sales, earnings, and cash growth will come from. Second, they should guide and review the selection of the proper management strategies. I have emphasized over and over again that management strategy guides implementation, because it can make an impact on each function and on the total management system. But the chief executive normally isn't close enough to the business to determine which management strategy offers the highest probability of success. The responsible manager is in a better position to determine the organization's unique strengths, competitive weaknesses, or environmental discontinuities, which can become the foundation of management strategy. But the chief executive can determine the viability of the selected option and can force the operating managers to provide workable alternatives. In addition, he or she must be sure that the preferred strategy fits the investment strategy and that it is backed up by implementation strategies and plans. Furthermore, the CEO is the only one who can assess how well the management team matches the strategy.

Finally, chief executives must monitor the situation and allocate rewards. They must ask: Is this strategy working? Will it yield the promised results? Will it require tuning, adjusting, or revisions? Operating managers are usually so enmeshed in running the business that they may forget what the strategy requires, or they may fail to see that results aren't being achieved as planned. Thus, the chief executive must establish a monitoring system to assess effectiveness. If the strategy is supposed to result in negative cash and short-term losses, but it is yielding profits instead, then he or she should question the reason. It may be a result of unique circumstances that permit simultaneous growth in sales, earnings, and cash. But it can also be the result of a strategy being aborted for the sake of short-term gains. If action is required to correct this situation, then the chief executive is responsible for initiating that action, which should be correlated with the rewards and measurement systems.

Chief executives need help just as everyone else does. They may not know what is expected of them and, even if they do, they may need help in making the tough decisions. Thus, the planner should help the chief executive make the decisions and communicate those decisions to the people who are responsible for implementation. The chief executive will also require help in identifying critical issues and in preparing for the review meetings. Without careful preparation, these sessions can degenerate into tactical rather than strategic reviews. This, in turn, will inhibit forward thinking and planning.

Factor III: Supporting the Total System

Given the proper commitment by planners and chief executives, the third critical factor is a supportive management system. Planning is only part of the system; I've also mentioned the need to have a consistent reward, measurement, and control system, and it is worth discussing these areas in more depth.

REWARDS AND MEASUREMENTS

Strategy focuses on the long term and on how results are to be achieved. It is counterproductive for you to have managers undertake an extensive, comprehensive planning exercise aimed at anticipating future trends and developing long-range options, only to reward them for immediate short-term results. If you pay for short-term results, you won't get long-term results.

Likewise, strategy deals with the "how," not just the results. Strategy denotes specific kinds of results and trade-offs. Sales growth normally requires a stabilized or declining income and a negative cash flow. A hold or defend strategy will permit earnings growth at the expense of sales, and harvesting strategies increase cash at the expense of sales. If a manager is supposed to be increasing share and enhancing his market position, but the results show increasing income and cash, then he or she should be asked why. If the manager's reasons can't be justified or if it is obvious that the strategy has been changed, then the manager should be penalized.

But the system shouldn't stop here; you should also find out how the results are being achieved. If you expect growth via innovation, and it is being achieved instead by pricing or manufacturing capacity, then this should also be examined, and if it can't be explained by environmental, competitive, or resource reasons, then the management should be punished. As I mentioned before, short-term results can be achieved by sacrificing long-term plans. It is possible to sell the company's birthright and thus to be nonviable in the long range.

Managers are smart and quickly determine what affects their compensation and promotional opportunities. Preaching planning but rewarding for no planning will result in no planning. Encouraging long-range thinking but paying on the basis of quarterly performance will result in quarterly, not long-range, results.

BUDGETS

Budgets are the financial expression of a strategy. If you don't have one integrated planning and budgeting system, you will not obtain consistent results. You should use planning assumptions and strategic programs to determine the results that you anticipate and the costs you expect to incur. This means that planning and financial managers must work together to develop both management tools. If the budgets call for different results than the plans, then one or the other must be changed.

RESOURCE ALLOCATION

One of the major reasons for implementing a strategic planning system is to guide a firm in allocating scarce financial and human resources. If the resource allocation system is separated from the strategic planning system, then one or the other will fail. Suppose that you expect share to be gained by adding capacity in advance of demand and that this calls for a plant expansion estimated to cost $25 million. Thus, plant expansion is a critical factor in successful implementation, and the expenditure of the $25 million is implicitly approved.

This doesn't mean that the resource allocation is automatic—the expenditure may not be approved, or only half the required amount may be expended. This means that capacity is added to meet, not to exceed, demand. As a result, the strategy won't be implemented as planned, and the investment and management strategies must be changed from growth to holding strategies.

There may be sufficient reasons for changing the allocation: lack of capital; uneconomical increase in the cost of capital; or even new data that have resulted in a reassessment of the attractiveness of the market, the industry, or the potential yields. Changes will occur, and this should be reflected in your strategic thrust.

Summary

In conclusion, I have attempted to highlight what it takes to move a strategy into action plans. This includes paying attention to changes required in the key functional programs and strategies, and examining how they fit in with the manufacturing, management, and business systems. Perfection and exact matching is impossible, but discontinuities must be considered in the timing and execution of the strategies.

10

Conclusions and Directions for Use

IMPLEMENTATION is what strategy is all about. You can't be satisfied with a theory, a system, or even a strategy that is creative, but isn't viable. Strategy must cover all bases, and must terminate with action programs.

In closing, I thought it might be useful to review all the key questions that I have covered in this book. This can also serve as a guide to using the approach that I have described.

1. What kind of business do you wish to have in the future?

This will give you a mission and a direction for the future, and will provide the guidelines for all the key managers.

2. Are there any unique factors in the micro-, macro-, or competitive environment that may have contributed to your past successes or failures? What are these factors, and do you believe that they will continue in the future?

This is really the essence of your environmental analysis and the cause of whether you change your mission and past strategy. It should be comprehensive and updated periodically, but only in the depth required to analyze critical factors.

3. What are the criteria that you have used and plan to use in the future to set investment priorities? Have they been sales- or profitability-based, or do they include other qualitative criteria?

This should help you determine what your priorities have been in the past and what they will be in the future. Unless you have set your criteria before making investment strategy decisions, your results will be fuzzy and confusing to the organization.

4. How have you segmented your business in the past, and how do you plan to do so in the future?

Segmentation is crucial to portfolio management. It will help you to explain your investment priorities and to spot any unserved but potentially attractive segments.

5. For each segment, what is your current assessment about its position and attractiveness? What will it be if you continue the same strategy? Where do you wish to be in the future?

These questions enable you to describe the degree, purpose, and timing of your investment strategies. The greater the change in position, the more complex the task will be, and the more investment of time, money, and manpower will be required.

6. What will be the leading thrust or driver that will enable you to achieve your investment goals and objectives?

This should be the result of a strength that you have, an obvious competitive weakness, or a discontinuity in the marketplace or in the total environment. I have dedicated the majority of this book to this topic, since I believe that it is the link between investment and implementation strategy and that this is the stage where there are many options and where creativity can yield the greatest payoff. The management strategy determines the nature of your functional implementation strategies.

7. What must be done in engineering, marketing, and manufacturing to successfully implement the strategy?

*This yields functional guidelines that describe the kinds of programs in each functional area. I have illustrated several of these, but you must think through the implications of **each** investment and management strategy.*

8. What must be changed in order to satisfy the guidelines?

This compares the guidelines with your current programs, and evaluates major changes in each segment. When surveyed across segments, it depicts the total impact on the entire business and enables you to assess total viability.

9. How will changes be achieved?

This helps you evaluate specific action items. Again, creativity and analysis will permit you to determine the extent of expenditures and costs and the timing of rewards. It provides action alternatives.

10. Will management and management systems fit the strategy, or must additional changes be made?

This forces a final, objective determination of viability, including an evaluation of you and your management team.

These ten questions can help you begin to formulate a total strategy. They summarize the essence of this book and will help you manage successfully—through the use of strategic planning.

INDEX

A&P, 164
Abbott Labs, 138
ABC budgeting systems, 111
acquisitions
  change affected by, 26, 27
  in executive-driven strategies,
    154–161
  of innovating companies, 142
Addressograph-Multigraph, 82,
  132
Admiral, 132
advertising
  coop, 90
  in demand-influencing
    strategies, 81, 82
  aggressive-pricing strategies,
    84–86
Air Bus Corporation, 151
air conditioners, 124
aircraft, 132
airlines, 85
Alcan Aluminum, 116
Allis-Chalmers, 97, 160
Allis-Fiat, 97, 160

Amana, 27, 127
Amax, 156
American Locomotive, 131
American Motors, 97
American Optical, 138
American Telephone and Tele-
  graph Company, 153
Anheuser-Busch, 81
applications, in service/appli-
  cation-directed strategies,
    92–96
ARCO, 116
Arcouettes, 109
Argentina, 118
Arthur D. Little Associates, 38
AT&T, 153
Atari, 158
attractiveness of investments de-
  termining, 49–53
  use of screens for, 54–56
automobiles
  catalytic converters for, 137
  innovation in, 128, 132–133,
    140

automobiles (cont.)
    material supplies for, 112–113
    model changes in, 127
Avis, 90, 158, 162

Babcock & Wilcox, 140, 159
backward integration, 53, 114–
    116, 118–119, 159
Baldwin (locomotives), 131
banks, as information sources,
    40–41
barter, 151–152
Bausch & Lomb, 138
B. Dalton Bookseller, 28
Beatrice Foods, 154–155, 161
Bell, Alexander Graham, 135,
    153
Bell & Howell, 164
Bell Labs, 139
Bell Telephone, 153
Beneficial Finance Company, 90
Bergdorf Goodman, 98
Bic, 77–78, 128
Bich, Marcel, 77, 78
boards of directors, 217–218
Borden, 155
Boston Consulting, 38, 46
Bowman, 86
breakeven points
    high, in capacity-based
        strategies, 106–107
    pricing strategies for, 84
Broadway Department Stores,
    98
budgets, 222
building products, 133
Burroughs, 93, 129
business magazines, 41
business managers, 69
business schools, as information
    sources, 40

Business Systems Technology,
    85–86

Cadillac, 83
Canada Dry, 90
Canadian General Electric, 157
Canadian Westinghouse, 157
capacity
    in manufacturing decisions,
        186, 188
    in production-based strat-
        egies, 8, 169, 171
capacity-based strategies, 105–
    107
capital
    leasing and, 147
    in process/equipment innova-
        tion-driven strategies, 108
    scarcity of, 12, 32
capital-intensive markets, 105–
    106
Carter Hawley Hale, 97–98
cash cows, 133
cash flow, in determining at-
    tractiveness of investments,
    52
change
    anticipation of, 23–25
    conditions affecting, 25–33
    in environment, capitalizing
        on, 65
    in segmentation or scope,
        97–98
    in strategy review, 212, 226
    technological, in determining
        attractiveness of invest-
        ments, 51–52
chief executive officers (CEOs)
    investment strategy decisions
        made by, 68, 69

production-based strategies and, 112
role in planning of, 217–221
Chile, 118
Coca-Cola, 156
color television, 127, 134
Combustion Engineering, 140
competition
changes in, 27–29
in determining attractiveness of investments, 50–51
in follow strategies, 139–143
increase in, 12–13
innovation to discourage, 128–130
leapfrogging over, 130–134
mergers and acquisitions to reduce, 157–158
in need/want identification strategies, 78
responses to, 182
understanding motivation of, 58–59
weaknesses of, 63–65
Composite Microcircuits, 164
computers
competition in, 85–86
expenses of, 52
innovation by IBM in, 129–130
leasing of, 64, 147–149
small and micro-, 140
see also IBM
Conference Board, The, 38
consignment selling, 9, 150
consortiums, 159–160
consultants, as information sources, 36–39
Container Corporation of America, 26, 156
Continental Oil, 116

contribution margin, 68*n.*
control
in distribution/dealer-focused strategies, 89–91
in high-pricing strategies, 87
Control Data, 129, 163
coop-advertising, 90
Corning Glass, 138, 160
corporate staffs, *see* staffs
cost of money, 45
costs
of data processing equipment and software, 52
in learning curve theory, 86
in low-pricing strategies, 88
Creative Strategies, Inc., 37
creativity, in implementation strategies, 67
credit cards, 149
Crosley, 117
Curtiss-Wright, 132
customer franchises, 81–82
customers
characteristics of, in attractiveness screens, 55
conditions affecting change in, 25–27
in demand-influencing strategies, 81–82
innovation-based strategies and, 123–124
in leasing arrangements, 147, 148
in need/want identification strategies, 76, 79
payment terms for, 149–152
in present corporate status, 21
in process/equipment innovation-driven strategies, 108–109

customers (cont.)
  in service/application-directed
    strategies, 93–96
data processing equipment
  expenses of, 52
  see also computers
Datsun, 97
Dayton-Hudson Properties, 28
dealers
  in distribution/dealer-focused
    strategies, 88–92
  in high-pricing strategies, 87
  see also distributors
decision making, 44–72
  in manufacturing, 185–189
  in marketing, 189–196
defending strategies, 304, 170–
    173
  marketing-based strategies
    for, 100
  promotion in, 184–185, 188–
    189, 191–195
defend-via-promotion strategies,
    184–185, 188–189
  marketing decisions for,
    191–195
Defibrator, 109
demand
  in capacity-based strategies,
    105–106
  in defensive strategies, 170–
    171
  growth options in, 168
  innovation to increase, 128
demand-influencing strategies,
    80–88
demographic change, 25
department stores, 85
deployment strategies, 119–122

depth, in implementation
    strategies, 181–182
DiMaggio, Joe, 81
discounters, 30, 85
dispositions, 161–164
distribution, changes in net-
    works for, 30
distribution/dealer-focused
    strategies, 88–92
  defensive, 171
  growth options in, 168, 169
  marketing decisions in, 190–
    191
distribution/deployment/readi-
    ness-to-serve strategies, 6
distributors
  brands created by, 117-118
  marketing decisions and,
    190–191
  see also dealers
diversification
  change affected by, 26
  to reduce overdependence,
    155–157
divestitures, 161–164
divestment strategies, 4–5
  management strategies in
    combination with, 174–175
  marketing-based strategies
    for, 101
Dow Chemical, 115
drug industry, 138
Du Pont Company
  growth-via revolutionary-de-
    sign strategy used by, 185
  high-pricing strategy used by,
    83
  innovation by, 5–6, 138
  materials cost-reduction
    research by, 113

new markets developed by, 134

Teflon and Silvertone developed by, 77

Eagle-Picher Industries, Inc., 78

Eastman Kodak, 124, 130, 132, 136

economy, in investment strategies, 53

Edison, Thomas Alva, 135, 138, 153, 214

Edison General Electric Company, 153, 158

efficiency-based strategies, 110–112

Electric Bond & Share Corporation, 153

electric lamps, 124, 135, 138

Electrophonics, 116

Emerson Electric, 111–112

employees, sales of companies to, 163–164

engineering, in marketing decisions, 189–190

engineering departments, 34–35

decisions influenced by, 181

value engineering by, 113–114

engineering strategies, 10, 184–185

checking guidelines against reality in, 201–202

in harvesting-via-high-pricing strategies, 207, 209

environment

capitalizing on changes in, 65

competitive, in determining attractiveness of investments, 50–51

conservation features for, 127–128

innovation opportunities created by, 137

in present corporate status, 19–20, 225

equipment

in implementation strategies, 183

in process/equipment innovation-driven strategies, 107–110

equity ownership, 152–153

Ethan Allen Furniture Co., 122

exclusivity, 182–183

executive-driven strategies, 9, 154–164

defensive, 172, 173

growth options in, 170

management skills for, 216

executive talent, 146–164

exiting strategies, 4–5

dispositions in, 161–164

management strategies in combination with, 174–175

marketing-based strategies for, 101

expropriations, 118

Exxon, 156–167

facilities

in implementation strategies, 183

in manufacturing decisions, 186

Fair Trade laws, 87

federal government, *see* government

Fiat, 97, 160

Fibreboard Corporation, 162

finances
    changes in, 32–33
    in determining attractiveness
        of investments, 52–53
    evaluating position in, 58
    financially driven strategies, *see*
        financial strategies
financial managers, 34
financial strategies, 11, 146–164
    defensive, 172, 173
    growth options in, 170
    management skills for, 216
financing, 146–164
Fisher (audio), 87
Fisher (automobile bodies), 115
flexibility, in manufacturing de-
    cisions, 186, 188–189, 202–
    203
follow strategies, 139–143, 169
    management skills for, 214
Food and Drug Administration
    (U.S.), 138
Forbes, 45, 46
Ford, Henry, 127, 135
Ford Motor Company
    credit organization of, 151
    model changes by, 127
    Philco purchased by, 117
    rotary engine development
        program of, 132
    small-car competition to, 64,
        140
foreign competitors
    advantages of, 28, 40
    redefining markets by, 96–97
    understanding motivation of,
        59
foreign countries
    barter and local manufacture
        in, 151–152

dealing with, in backward in-
    tegration, 118–119
foreign markets, implementa-
    tion strategies for, 10
forward integration, 159
franchising, 9
    in distribution/dealer-focused
        strategies, 89–91
Frigidaire, 117
Frost and Sullivan, 38
funding
    in growth via innovation
        strategies, 201, 202
    in implementation strategies,
        183

gap analysis, 71
G. D. Searle, 138
General Atomics, 133, 157
General Electric, 117
    computers by, 129
    in creation of RCA, 138
    innovation by, 127
    jet engines by, 132
    nuclear reactors by, 140
    as successor to Edison GE,
        153
General Foods, 81
General Mills, 81
General Motors
    backward integration in, 115
    credit organization of, 150
    Frigidaire purchased by, 117
    locomotives by, 131
    model changes introduced by,
        127
    rotary engine development
        program of, 132
    small-car competition to, 64,
        140

geographic/segment redefinition
  strategies, 96–99
  defensive, 171
  growth options in, 169
Getty Oil, 157
Gillette, 78, 128
Goodrich, 164
government
  capitalizing on regulatory
    changes caused by, 65
  changes in, 30–31
  as customer, 26
  Fair Trade laws of, 87
  funding from, 183, 201, 202
  IBM pressured by, 149
  innovation in responses to,
    137, 140–141
  manufacturing and selling
    regulated by, 12
  mergers and acquisitions regu-
    lated by, 158
  production-focused strategies
    forced by regulation of, 108
  publications of, 41
Government Printing Office,
  U.S., 41
Griffiths, Ed, 111
growth, as investment criterion,
  46–48
growth strategies, 3, 167–170
growth via innovation strategies
  checking guidelines against
    reality in, 201–207
  marketing decisions for, 191,
    192, 194–195
growth-via-revolutionary-design
  strategies, 184, 185, 188
  management skills for, 214
GSW, Ltd., 157
guarantees, 87

guidelines, checking reality
  against, 201–207
Gulf, 133

Haloid, 132
Halston, 90
H & R Block, 137
Hardwick, 118
Hartford Insurance, 158
harvesting strategies, 4
  high pricing for, 207–209
  marketing-based strategies
    for, 100
  marketing management in,
    172–173
Hewlett-Packard, 28
high-pricing strategies, 83–84
  harvesting in, 207–209
  resources necessary for, 87
holding strategies, 3–4, 170–173
  marketing-based strategies
    for, 100
Holiday Inn, 90
Holt, Renfrew, 98
Honeywell, Inc., 78, 129
Houghton, Amory, 160
Household Finance Company,
  90
Howard Johnson's, 89
Hunt-Wesson, 90
hurdle rates, 45–46

IBM
  applications developed by, 94
  Business Systems Technology
    competing with, 85–86
  evaluation of success of, 19
  facilities of, 183
  forced to sell to Control Data,
    163

IBM (cont.)
  innovation by, 129–130
  leasing by, 147, 149
  marketing strategy of, 6, 21
  micro-computers by, 139–140
  service and applications
    strengths of, 65
  typewriters of, 132
  weakness of competitors of, 64
  see also computers
Illinois Central Corporation, 26
images
  in demand-influencing strat-
    egies, 81–83
  in implementation strategies,
    182
implementation of strategies,
    224–226
implementation strategies,   2,
    9–11, 167–196
  development of, 65–68
  responsibilities for, 13–14, 69
industrial customers, 26
  need/want identification
    strategies for, 79
industry associations, 39–40
industry factors, in present cor-
    porate status, 22–23
innovation
  exclusivity in, 183
  in need/want identification
    strategies, 77
  in process/equipment innova-
    tion-driven strategies, 107–
    110
  productivity counter to, 187
innovation-based strategies,   7,
    123–143
  growth via, 191, 192, 194–195,
    201–207
  management skills for, 214

instant photography, 124, 130
integration
  of acquired or merged com-
    panies, 161
  backward, 53, 114–116, 118–
    119, 159
  in harvesting-via-high-pricing
    strategies, 207–209
  for need/want identification
    strategies, 79
intelligence strategies, 193
Intercollegiate Case Clearing
    House, 40
interest rates
  hurdle rate determined by, 45
  in payment terms, 150–151
Interlock Furniture, 164
International Business Machines
    Corporation, *see* IBM
International Paper, 84
inventions
  creating markets for, 135–136
  see also innovation
inventories
  in deployment strategies, 119
  needed in demand-influ-
    encing strategies, 82
investment firms, 40
investment strategies, 1–5
  determining attractiveness of
    investments for, 49–53
  evaluation of position in,
    56–60
  management strategies in
    combination with, 167–175
  marketing-based strategies
    matched with, 99–101
  matrixes used in, 60–61
  priorities in, 44–49, 225
  responsibilities for, 13, 68–
    69

use of attractiveness screens
in, 54–56
Iran, 115
ITT, 158, 162

Japan, 96
barter by, 151
production-based strategies
in, 106–111, 116, 119
radios manufactured in, 132
joint development, 116
joint venturing, 159–160
J. Ray McDermott, 159

Kayakas, 109
Kidde Corporation, 156
K-Mart, 91
Kodak, 124, 130, 132, 136
Korvettes, 85
Kresge, 91

Land, Edward, 214
leadership, in innovation-based
strategies, 125–139, 169
leapfrogging, 130–134, 169
learning curve theory, 86
pricing by, 168
leasing, 9
of computers, 64
in financially driven strategies,
147–149
increase in, 94
Lechmere Tire & Sales, 28
legislation
Fair Trade, 87
innovation in responses to,
137, 140–141
manufacturing and selling regulated by, 12
see also government
Lenox, 122

Levitt (houses), 162
licensing
in distribution/dealer-focused
strategies, 91
in innovation-based strategies,
136, 138–140
for local manufacture, 152
of patents, 51
Lloyds, 116
load levelling, 84
location
in attractiveness screens, 54
see also geographic/segment
redefinition strategies
locomotives, 131
logistics of manufacturing decisions, 187–189
low-pricing strategies, 84–86
resources necessary for, 88

McCall's Patterns, 90
McDonald's 19, 89
McGraw-Edison, 118
McKinsey, 38
macroenvironment, 20, 53
magazines, 41
Magnavox, 157
maintenance
in capacity-based strategies,
107
in service/application-directed
strategies, 95
management
of acquired or merged companies, 161
in implementation strategies,
11
levels of responsibility of,
13–14
matrix organization of, 79–
80

management (cont.)
  role of, in planning and exe-
    cuting strategies, 213–217,
    226
  strategy decision making by,
    68–71
  in support systems, 221–223
management by objectives, 45
management strategies, 2, 5–9
  chief executive officers' re-
    views of, 220
  investment strategies in com-
    bination with, 167–175
  responsibilities for, 13, 69
  selection of, 61–65
managers
  operating, as information
    source, 34–35
  reporting to chief executive
    officers, 219–220
manufacturing
  decisions in, 185–189
  local, in payment terms, 151–
    152
manufacturing-based strategies,
    8, 104, 110–112
  checking guidelines against
    reality in, 202–204
  in harvesting-via-high-pricing
    strategies, 207–209
  management skills for, 215–
    216
manufacturing departments, 34,
    35
manufacturing processes, in de-
    termining attractiveness of
    investments, 53
Marathon Oil, 157
Marconi Wireless Telegraph
    Co., Ltd., 138
Marcor Inc., 26, 156

marketing
  decisions in, 189–196
  evaluating position in, 57
  in implementation strategies,
    66
marketing-based strategies, 6–8,
    10–11, 101
  checking guidelines against
    reality in, 204–207
  defensive, 170–171
  growth options in, 168–169
  in harvesting-via-high-pricing
    strategies, 209
  management skills for, 214–
    215
marketing staffs, 34
markets
  in attractiveness screens,
    54–55
  capital-intensive, 105–106
  changes in, 27, 28
  in determining attractiveness
    of investments, 49–50
  development of, in demand-
    influencing strategies,
    80–81
  development of, in innova-
    tion-based strategies, 134–
    136
  foreign, 10
  in investment strategies, 3–5
  mergers and acquisitions to
    improve position in, 157–
    158
  in present corporate status,
    21
  redefining strategy for, 96–99
Masters, 86
materials, *see* supplies
matrixes, in investment
    strategies, 60–61

matrix management organization, 79–80
Matsushita, 97, 135, 157, 163
Max Factor, 90
Maytag, 83
Mazda, 132–133, 140
MCA/Philips, 140, 160
measurement, 220–222
Mercedes, 83
mergers
 change affected by, 26, 27
 in executive-driven strategies, 154–161
 with innovating companies, 142
microenvironment, 19
Midas, 26
Miller Brewing Company, 81
mining, 115, 159
Mr. Coffee, 80–81
Mobil, 26, 156
moderate-pricing strategies, 84
 resources necessary for, 88
MolyCorp, 156
monitoring systems, 220
Monroe Auto Equipment, 159
Monsanto Company, 116, 162
Montgomery Ward, 26, 156
motivation of competitors, understanding, 58–59
Motorola, 97, 132, 157

National Cash Register, 129
National Semiconductor, 78
NBC, 134
need/want identification strategies, 76–80
Neiman Marcus, 98
Nestle, 158
New York City, 26

no follow strategies, 141–143, 169
Norton Simon, 90, 158
nuclear power, 93, 133, 140
Nuclear Regulatory Commission (U.S.), 93

office machines, 132
Offshore Power Corporation, 160
oil industry, *see* petroleum industry
Oldsmobile, 87
operating managers, 34–35
 reporting to chief executive officers, 219–220
Organization of Petroleum Exporting Countries (OPEC), 22, 83
original equipment manufacturers (OEMs), 190
Owens-Corning Fiberglas, 138
Owens-Illinois, 138

Panasonic, 132
Pan Ocean Oil, 157
partnerships, 159–160
 for funding, 183
patents
 in innovation-based strategies, 7
 in investment strategies, 51
payment terms, 149–152
penetration strategies, 3
 marketing-based strategies for, 100
pensions, portable, 32–33
Pepsico, 90, 156
perceived value, 195–196
personal consulting, 36
Personna, 78

Petrie Shops, 111
petroleum industry
  backward integration in,
    114–115
  diversification in, 156–157
  joint development in, 116
  partnerships in, 159
Philco, 117, 132
Philip Morris, 78, 81
Philips
  audiocasette tapes of, 136
  facilities of, 183
  Magnavox purchased by, 157
  video recording by, 140, 160
Pizza Hut, 90
planning
  critical factors in, 217–223
  role of management in, 213–
    217
  see also strategies
Polaroid, 7, 124, 130
portfolio management, 142
position, evaluation of, 56–60
Pratt & Whitney, 132
pre-sales service, 93
price
  in defensive strategies, 171
  in growth strategies, 168, 169
  in marketing-driven
    strategies, 7
  umbrella, 101
pricing strategies
  demand influenced by, 83–86
  high, harvesting in, 207–209
  marketing decisions for,
    195–196
  resources necessary for, 86–88
priorities, setting of, 44–72
process/equipment innovation-
  driven strategies, 107–110
Procter and Gamble, 5, 81

product-based strategies, 169
  harvesting in, 173
product cycles, extending, 125–
  128
production
  evaluating position in, 58
  in implementation strategies,
    66
production-based strategies, 8,
  104–122
  defensive, 171, 173
  growth options in, 169
  management skills for, 215
productivity, in management
  decisions, 187–189
productivity-based strategies,
  110–112
products
  defensive strategies for, 171–
    173
  differentiation in, 7
  existing, adding new life to, 81
  increasing usage of, 94
  innovation in, 123–143
  management and planning of,
    189–190
  new, developing markets for,
    80–81
  standardization and differ-
    entiation between, 51–52
  use of, in attractiveness
    screens, 54
profitability, growth not equated
  with, 47
programs
  evaluation of, in implementa-
    tion strategies, 67–68
  supporting implementation
    strategies, 66
progress payments, 149–150
project managers, 80

promotional-based strategies,
183
promotions
in defend-via-promotion strategy, 184–185, 188–189,
191–195
demand influenced by, 80–83
pruning, 161–164
pull strategies, 6
purchasing
in lease arrangements, 147
move from leasing to, 148–149
terms and conditions of,
149–152
purchasing behavior, 54

quality, in high-pricing strategies, 83, 87
Quasar, 97, 157, 163
"quick follow" strategies,
139–141, 169
management skills for, 214

radios, 132
Radio Shack, 91
Raytheon, 27
razors, 77–78, 128
RCA
color television introduced by,
127, 134
computers by, 129
founding of, 138
management of, 27, 111
radios by, 132
video recording by, 135, 140
readiness-to-serve strategies, 6,
119–122
marketing decisions for,
193–194
rebuilding, in investment
strategies, 4

reduction-of-share strategies,
100–101
regulation, *see* government;
legislation
Remington Rand, 64, 132
rentals
increasing usage of, 94
see also leasing
reputation, *see* images
research, in innovation-based
strategies, 138
research staffs, 35
resources
allocation of, 222–223
assessment of, in implementation strategies, 67
changes in supply of, 31–32
necessary for pricing
strategies, 86–88
needed for leasing, 148
responsibilities
in decision making, 68–71
designating, 13–14
returns on equity, 45
returns on investment, 52–53
returns on total capital, 45
Revco, 118
review of strategies, 71–72,
209–212
rewards, 220–222
Rhodesia, 31–32
Rockwell/Admiral, 118
Rockwell Microelectronics, 86,
98
Rohm & Haas, 162
Rolls Royce, 132
Royal, 132
Royal Dutch Shell, 116, 133, 157

sales
of companies, 163–164

sales (cont.)
  consignment, 9, 150
  in investment strategies, 3–4
sales strategies, 191–192
Sanyo, 157
Sarnoff, David, 27, 111
Sarnoff, Robert, 111
Savin Business Machines, 82
Schlitz, 81
Schwinn & Company, 89
scope
  changing, 97–98
  in implementation strategies,
    181–182
Sears, Roebuck and Co.
  credit purchases from, 149,
    150
  marketing-based strategies of,
    95, 98
  own brandnames used by, 82,
    116–117
  upgrading by, 28
  segmentation, 97–98, 181, 225
  see also geographic/segment
    redefinition strategies
semiconductors, 108
service
  in defensive strategies, 171
  in marketing-driven
    strategies, 6–7
  in service/application-directed
    strategies, 92–96, 168, 192–
    193
service/application-directed
    strategies, 92–96
  growth options in, 168
  marketing decisions for,
    192–193
Shell, 116, 133, 157
Sheraton, 87
Schick, 78

ships, factories on, 110
Siecor Optical Cables, 160
Siemens, 97, 160
Silvertone, 77
Skelley Oil, 157
skills
  assessment of, in implementa-
    tion strategies, 66–67
  management, compatible with
    strategies, 214–217
  in process/equipment innova-
    tion-driven strategies, 107–
    109
slow follow strategies, 141–143
Smith Corona, 132
Société Bic, 77
sociopolitical factors, in invest-
    ment strategies, 53
software
  applications of, 94
  expenses of, 52
solar energy, 140
Somerset Importers, 90
Sony, 97
  high-pricing strategy of, 83
  radios by, 132
  video recording by, 134–135,
    140
Soundesign, 116
sourcing-based strategies, 8,
    116–118
South Africa, 31–32
Southwest Airlines, 85
Soviet Union, 32
Sperry & Hutchinson, 164
Sperry Rand, 129
spin-offs, 163
SRI (Stanford Research Insti-
    tute), 37
staffs
  as information sources, 34–36

reporting to chief executive officers, 219–220
standardization
in marketing-driven strategies, 7–8
product differentiation in, 51–52
Standard Oil of California, 156
Stanford Research Institute (SRI), 37
status, in high-pricing strategies, 87
steel industry, 109
stock and investment firms, 40
Stolman Corporation, 79
Stouffer's, 158
strategic analysis
decision making in, 44–72
information sources for, 34–41
strategic thinking, 17–41
strategies
checking against reality, 201–207
critical factors for success in, 127–223
designating responsibilities for, 13–14
financial and executive, 146–164
implementation, 167–196
importance of, 11–13
innovation-based, 123–143
marketing-based, 75–101
production-based, 104–122
review of, 71–72, 209–212
role of management in planning and executing of, 213–217
types of, 1–11
Studebaker, 156

sufficiency
in implementation strategies, 182–183
in manufacturing decisions, 186–189
suppliers, long-term contracts with, 114
supply
in high-pricing strategies, 83
in production-based strategies, 8
of resources, changes in, 31–32
supply-assurance strategies, 112–119
support systems, 221–223

Tandy Corporation, 91
Target Discount Stores, 28
taxes, 115, 137
Team Central, Inc., 28
technology
change in, in determining attractiveness of investments, 51–52
changes caused by, 29–30
competition in, 140
evaluating position in, 57–58
management skills and, 214
in present corporate status, 22
Teflon, 77
telephones, 94, 135
television, 127, 134–135, 140
Tenneco, 110, 159, 160
terms of payment, 149–152
Texas Instruments, 28, 86, 98
Thompson-Houston, 158
Toyota, 97
trade associations, 39–40
traffic functions, 188
transistors, 139

transportable factories, 109–110
turnover, in sales, 111
typewriters, 132

umbrella prices, 101
Underwood, 132
Union Camp, 105
Union Corporation, 138
Union Oil, 156
unions, 53
United States, *see* government
United Technologies, 159
universities, as information
    sources, 40
utilities, 153
utilization
    in capacity-based strategies,
        106–107
    in production-based strategies,
        8
    in service/application-directed
        strategies, 95–96

value engineering, 113–114
video recording, 134–135, 140
VLSI semiconductors, 108
Volkswagen, 64, 97
volume
    in distribution/dealer-focused
        strategies, 92
    in learning curve theory, 86
    pricing strategies for, 84

Walker Manufacturing, 159
Warner Communications, 158–
    159
Warner-Lambert, 138
warranties, 87
Warren-Teed   Pharmaceuticals,
    162
Warwick, 157
watches, 78
Watson, Thomas, Sr., 21
Weinstock's Stores, 98
West Germany, 108
Westinghouse
    appliance business sold by,
        163
    nuclear reactors by, 110, 140
    Offshore Power Corporation
        and, 160
    RCA founding and, 138
Westport, Connecticut, 29
Weyerhauser, 105, 109
White Consolidated (WCI),
    163
Wiltex, 148
workforce, changes in, 32–33
Worthington, 156

Xerography, 132
Xerox, 7, 82, 94, 147

Zenith, 135, 140, 155